How to Watc

10

THE GINGER SERIES

OTHER TITLES IN THE GINGER SERIES

01 How to Watch a Game of Rugby
    Spiro Zavos

02 How to Gaze at the Southern Stars
    Richard Hall

03 How to Listen to Pop Music
    Nick Bollinger

04 How to Pick a Winner
    Mary Mountier

05 How to Drink a Glass of Wine
    John Saker

06 How to Catch a Fish
    Kevin Ireland

07 How to Look at a Painting
    Justin Paton

08 How to Read a Book
    Kelly Ana Morey

09 How to Catch a Cricket Match
    Harry Ricketts

how to watch a bird
a bird
steve braunias

AWA PRESS

First edition published in 2007 by
Awa Press, 16 Walter Street,
Wellington, New Zealand

National Library of New Zealand Cataloguing-in-Publication Data
Braunias, Steve.
How to watch a bird / Steve Braunias.
(The ginger series ; 10)
ISBN 978-0-9582629-6-5
1. Bird watching. I. Title. II. Series: Ginger series: (Wellington, N.Z.)
598.07234—dc 22

The publisher and author gratefully acknowledge the assistance of the
Auckland Museum in providing photographs from the Buddle Collection.

Typesetting by Jill Livestre, Archetype
Printed by Printlink, Wellington
Printed on environmentally friendly and chlorine-free Munken paper.
This book is typeset in Walbaum

www.awapress.com

To Emily and Minka

THE PHOTOGRAPHS

One of the heroes of this book is Major
Geoffrey Buddle. Awarded the Distinguished
Service Order, the Military Cross and the
White Eagle of Serbia for his bravery in
World War I, he was gassed in France and not
expected to live when he returned to New
Zealand. But he survived, and travelled with
his friends Edgar Stead and Major Rodney
Wilson to study birds in some of the most
remote corners of New Zealand. Buddle died
in 1951, the year that A.H. & A.W. Reed
published his exquisite book of photography,
Bird Secrets. Many of the photographs repro-
duced in this book come from that classic
work. The other photographs are also held in
the Buddle Collection at Auckland Museum.
Faded, bewitching, timeless, the photographs
reveal his lifelong love of birds. The captions
are as he wrote them.

ABOUT THE AUTHOR

STEVE BRAUNIAS is a senior writer and columnist with *The Sunday Star-Times*, and winner of numerous national journalism awards. *Fool's Paradise*, his book of selected columns, won Best First Book of Non-Fiction at the 2002 Montana Book Awards. He has been the editor of *Capital Times*, feature writer at *Metro*, deputy editor at the *Listener*, and is a contributing writer to TV One's *Eating Media Lunch* and *The Unauthorised History of New Zealand*.

Red-billed Gull
following the yacht
off the North Cape,
6.1.47

Summer

I T WAS OUR first summer together. We had gone on a road trip up north over Christmas — five motels in seven nights, wet towels drying on the back seat. It was barbecue weather, New Zealand with sand in its hair, barefoot on hot pavements, undressed and dazed and unshaved, on vacation, gone fishing, fed and watered, half asleep, on good terms with itself, happy, setting off fireworks to see in the New Year.

There was an afternoon watching something spectacular — on the beach at Ruakaka, where a flock of gannets smashed into the water and came back up with fish. That was such a dazzling sight, but every day was dazzling. When I think about that week, I remember the sun high in the sky, the car strolling along on dusty roads between quiet fields of yellow short-haired grass. In the towns, fat kids stuffed themselves with ice-blocks and fizz outside dairies, and light breezes whisked dust down the middle of the street. The towns gave way to lines of gum trees peeling in the sun. You could go hours without hearing a sound in our lazy sensual isles at the end of the world.

I was in love with New Zealand and in love with Emily. Summer with Emily — that's mainly what I remember. Emily swimming, Emily sleeping, Emily driving her passenger.

We went back to work. I don't remember much about that. Life was with Emily at my rented apartment near a bay, with Emily at her rented apartment in the city. Late one night, I stepped out on to her balcony for a cigarette. It was towards the end of January. A summer's evening, long past dark, the air finally cooling and only as warm as toast after the fructifying heat of daylight hours. I stood and smoked, and then a bird flew past right in front of my snoot. You could say it was any old bird — it was that common, unloved scavenger, a black-backed gull, a big quiet thing, in no apparent hurry, slowly flying past, then slowly circling back again, and its silent, sudden appearance in darkness was stranger than anything happening down below among the traffic and the street lights.

It felt like a jolt. The gull had come by so close; in the darkness its white body had glowed like a lamp swinging on a porch. No doubt it had good reason to be going about its business on an obscure hour in the middle of downtown Auckland. What business? Back then, I would have thought that God only knew, and it turned out that I was right – God had known, in an earlier summer, 1968–69 to be precise, when the roof-nesting habits of black-backed gulls in downtown Auckland were studied by Graham Turbott, a lovely man who at 92 is the godfather of New Zealand ornithology.

Turbott's report on the gulls, published in a 1969 issue of *Notornis*, referred to the observation of four pairs of birds at breeding sites around the city. Two chicks were hatched from a bulky nest of grass and paper on the roof of the Old Oxford Theatre on Queen Street; one chick hatched but died on the roof of a hot-water tank on top of the Chief Post Office. Chicks were seen to depart the nest in mid January from the roof of the Magistrate's Court in Kitchener Street. At 24 Cook Street, according to a Miss J. Walker who 'kept a constant watch' on the gulls' nest in the gutter at the edge of the roof, a young bird, fully fledged at six weeks, left with both its parents on February 7; it had hatched from its manger in the gutter on Christmas Day.

The bird I saw was an adult, and probably still feeding its chick. Black-backed gulls – *Larus dominicianus* – nest in large colonies of up to several thousand pairs in the greater outdoors of the coast, but form solitary two-parent families in the city. They can swallow a cutlet of mutton whole. Offal is also acceptable.

The oldest recorded New Zealand black-back was a been-there, ate-that 28 years old. In its adult prime, the bird isn't a bad looker; it has yellow eyes and a bright red smear on its bill. But it takes two moults and nearly three years before juveniles assume the smooth whiteness that glows like a lamp. Young black-backs are among the most unpleasant things on wings. A lot of people mistake these large mottled brutes for some other kind of bird, and refuse to throw them scraps, out of distaste for their appearance. No one should be in the least surprised that these plug-ugly thugs don't get any sex until they are at least four years old.

I didn't know any of these things when I saw the black-back brush past my nose that summer's evening. I didn't know nothing about any birds. But when I caught sight of that one bird, felt the jolt it gave, that white flash in the black night, I was bowled over with happiness, and I thought: birds, everywhere. Summer in New Zealand fills with so much light that we become the land of the long white page. Every corner, every margin is filled with birds.

As a weekly magazine columnist since 1999, a lot of my writing has imagined different kinds of maps of New Zealand – of the things and pleasures that are right in front of us, that tell almost a secret history of the place, that maybe even reveal an emotional truth about the place. And so I've written a series of columns about hot springs. About steak. About mangroves. About tearooms. About things and pleasures you can find all across the country, from one town or shore to the next, forming a grid. I now wanted very much to write about birds.

Birds of the city and town, on lawn and roof. Birds of the bush and the shore and the wide open sea. Paddock, lakeside, riverbank, wharf, telephone wire, bridge, swamp, alp: everywhere, birds. Migrants, most dramatically the bar-tailed godwit, flying for seven, eight days from Alaska without rest, until landfall in New Zealand. Common or garden varieties, like the blackbird and the house sparrow, brought to New Zealand by England's homesick colonists. Native endemics, some still around — the tui, the takahe — and some wiped out, extinct, ghosts of another time — the huia, the moa. Birds that have come and gone and may come again, such as the red-necked avocet, quite possibly the most amazing bird to ever grace these shores, but seldom straying here from its breeding grounds across the ditch in Brisbane. Birds nesting under bridges; birds nesting in sand. Big fat birds, birds as small as full stops, as a row of dots ...

Could you be a bit more specific? Yes, in time. 2006 became my year of birds. I took down names. I saw birds I never knew existed. I became fascinated with birds that no longer existed, and with the literature of birds, with the social history of watching birds in New Zealand.

I learned things. I shared pleasures. I saw another New Zealand, a particular geography where its borders and centres were defined by birds — a feathered New Zealand. And I saw another kind of New Zealander, their lives transformed, consumed, by birds.

I loved seeing what they had seen, that year, and years before. I loved discovering a simple truth: to watch a bird is to see the world in a completely different way.

I watched the birds — 'Beside us,' as poet Matthew Arnold wrote, 'but alone' — and I watched the watchers. I watched the world of New Zealand with refreshed eyes. It was a great privilege. I felt alert, awed, alive. And it was strange timing the way that marvellous year coincided with something else in my life, something amazing, that happened along the way.

Gannet on the nest,
Waiheke, 2.10.46

An early bird

BIRDS ARE SO obvious, and so apart. They have their own New Zealand. We all know about the famous roosts – the gannet colonies at Muriwai and Cape Kidnappers, the albatrosses and penguins in Dunedin, the muttonbirds in Foveaux Strait. We care about the continued presence of our emblematic birds such as the kiwi and the kakapo lurking in the bush. It's a very good thing to go to sleep in our houses with the familiar sound of the morepork hooting through the night. For years, my favourite bird-watching spot in the whole country was where I could see the 40 or so pairs of little shags that nested in a stand of trees above a pond by the kiosk in Christchurch's Hagley Park from June through to January.

Lovely. But this is the notion of birds fitting in with the rest of us – birds lucky enough to be left to their own devices, survivors of modern, peopled life. Most of us think of birds as something in the background. They flit and they pace, they nest and they sing, bystanders of the air, second-class citizens, largely unnoticed. They may as well be grass.

One afternoon in February, I bowled along to the hall of birds at the Auckland Museum. Replica of a moa here, replica of a likewise extinct and distinctly ponderous New Zealand giant penguin there. All well and good, most interesting, but what made it shattering was that my visit to the museum was the first time I learned a simple fact which I assume so many schoolchildren have learned: that New Zealand, uniquely, spectacularly, was birdland. Until the arrival of humans, birds had the run of the place. They were here when the New Zealand archipelago set itself loose from Gondwanaland about 80 million years ago. The theory is that the moa and the kiwi, our famous ratites, flightless birds, just stood there as the land separated. Cutely, the theory's known as Moa's Ark – New Zealand was a cargo ship, and the ratites went along for the ride.

More birds arrived, by wing and wind, and it appears likely that most of our native species, such as the tui, are actually ancient Australians. Since when – 40 million years ago? Twenty million? Is it possible the kiwi also flew from Australia, and then adapted to life in New Zealand as a flightless ground predator?

Birds are small-boned; the fossil record is lousy. I suspect the lack of evidence acts as a balm to Don Hadden, a former teacher at the Christian school Middleton Grange in Christchurch, and one of our most knowledgeable bird photographers. His book *99 New Zealand Birds* quotes Genesis: 'God created ... every winged bird according to its kind.'

Middleton Grange goes in for the nonsense of a young Earth created by God only 8000 years ago. The rest of us can thank birds for explaining the way the world really works: the light bulb of the theory of evolution that first flashed over Darwin's head was courtesy of his study of Galapagos Island finches. There is an exhilarating passage in his book *Journal of the Beagle*, written long before he came up with the single greatest idea ever to occur to the human mind, where he muses on the different beak structure of 13 finches: 'Seeing this ... diversity in one small, intimately related group of birds, one might really fancy that from an original paucity of birds in this archipelago, one species had been taken and modified for different ends.'

The glint of that light bulb over his head came as Darwin sailed on the *Beagle* towards New Zealand. He spent the Christmas of 1835 here. He hated it, couldn't wait to leave. Q: What do you think of New Zealand,

Mr Darwin? A: Rubbish. But he had unknowingly set foot on one of the world's great natural laboratories. In 1839, Richard Owen, an English biologist and one of the few men the kindly Darwin detested, identified the fossil remains of a giant bird as the moa. Talk about your 'modified for different ends': the moa and other flightless birds evolved to take the place of land mammals, and found their food on the forest floor.

'As time passed,' wrote that emotional Victorian ornithologist James Drummond, 'the birds that had come down to these parts found they possessed a land of surpassing goodness.' It's long been supposed that mammals were absent in New Zealand, although the discovery in late 2006 of three small bones in Central Otago proved that a mammal species had existed here, about 16 million years ago. 'This ranks up there with the discovery of the first moa bones, and the first dinosaur bones in New Zealand,' Te Papa's fossil curator, Alan Tennyson, told *The New Zealand Herald*. Really? It's true that the find exploded a myth. But steady on. The mammal was about the size of a mouse. Tennyson: 'This shows the land of birds is not true. However, if land mammals were this size, the story may not have changed much…'

In a land without predators, birds never had it so good. Strangely, no photos exist from that period, but you can see it imagined in those fantastic paintings, dripping with ancient ooze and populated with outrageous bird-people, by Bill Hammond. The Christchurch painter has said the inspiration for his famous series came from a visit to the subantarctic Auckland Islands in 1991. 'I saw a New Zealand before there were men, women, dogs and possums.'

He saw a New Zealand where birds were right out in front. That stern Victorian ornithologist James Drummond seemed to find this a deplorable state of affairs. 'Life was too easy for them; so many first neglected, and then lost, the power of flight, and dropped into an indolent way of doing things, which became their undoing.'

Actually, mankind became their undoing. We are often fed the line that early Maori formed a deep spiritual bond with the natural world, treated it with awe and respect. That line has quite a lot going for it. Probably the best instance is Margaret Orbell's book *Birds of Aotearoa: A Natural and Cultural History*, which reads like an ode to the assorted glorious harmonies between Maori and New Zealand's birds.

You won't read anything like that about the first European settlers. Ornithological literature tends to cast white colonists as a barbarian horde who sacked the land. They felled bush and drained swamps. They introduced predators. They shot birds for sport, or to collect the skins.

Shocking, disgraceful. But Maori hunting and Maori-introduced predators, including the rat and the dog, led to the extinction of all nine species of 'indolent' moa, various species of goose, duck, adzebill, rail, coot, the magnificent Haast's eagle, and other birds — in fact, the number far outweighs the avian species made extinct since the arrival of the first Europeans.

Point-scoring of this nature only conforms to the national pastime of separating every issue in New Zealand society to either side of a racial divide. Yes, the moa — with its estimated population of 187,590 reduced to precisely zero — fell victim to what Tim Flannery, author of *The Future Eaters*, calls 'the black hole' theory of extinction, meaning that they fell into that dark, bottomless pit known as the human gob. But much of New Zealand was still birdland when James Cook sailed into view. When the *Endeavour* entered Queen Charlotte Sound on 17 January 1770, the dawn chorus sang its head off — 'a melodious wild musick', as heard by the ship's naturalist, Joseph Banks.

The sound we hear now is an unplugged version. The catastrophe of two waves of human settlement has diminished bird populations, and forced many on to offshore islands. Over the past 50 years, efforts by conservationists have attempted, and sometimes succeeded, in bringing endangered birds back to the mainland, and in extreme cases back from the brink. Fantastic. We want them around. All birds make us feel happy, feel better about where we live, but the point is that's it's not about our feelings — it's actually about the birds.

I learned something the night I brought along an advance proof copy of *Extinct Birds of New Zealand*, a handsome new illustrated book published by Te Papa, to an Ornithological Society meeting in Auckland. If anyone wanted to have a look at it, I said, they were welcome. It proved attractive bait. Really, it was like bringing a crate of booze to AA. They flocked around it, they pawed at it, inspecting the pictures, reading out bits of text, cooing and cawing and sounding expert opinions. In short, they loved it. But as well as the noises of admiration for author Alan Tennyson and artist Paul Martinson, there were constant sighings. It was actually a sad gathering. They felt cheated. A stillness had entered the room: I was a messenger of death. These bird-watchers were looking at birds they would never see.

They had seen so many birds, handled their soft warm bodies, studied them in depth — they were fans of birds, they followed their careers, but it was an awful lot deeper than that. They craved life. A valuable lesson, and a good place for me to start learning how to watch a bird.

*Little Pied Shag on
her nest calls to her
mate, while a pair
of Big Black Shags
rest after feeding
young, Foxton,
27.11.42*

A good shag

IF YOU WANT to know how to watch a bird, what you do is borrow someone else's eyes. There are a few ways of going about this. The first and best way is to get a pair of binoculars. They really do feel like another person has moved in. Actually, they *are* another person, a bird-watcher's best friend. They do what you most want: they bring you closer to the bird.

The effect is quite staggering at first; after continued use, it's still quite staggering. I never get over it, always feel happily dazzled by that simple magic trick. As a form of media, binoculars even beat television.

Binoculars is a long, ungainly word, and no one who

goes bird-watching wastes time with all those syllables. The proper term is bins, just as the proper term for the next big step, a telescope, is scope. Scopes are wide-screen. They cost serious money. You have to cart them around. I travel light. Also, I'm cheap.

Bins are like a portable TV. As such, my favourite programme in the autumn and winter of 2006 took place at the bay around the corner from my apartment. I trotted down there four or five days a week, at low tide and high tide, the tide shuffling in and the tide shuffling out on a mud-flat next to the Auckland harbour bridge. There were South Island pied oystercatcher – SIPO they're called – and kingfisher, and three species of shag, and a pair of white-faced heron. There was also a home-less guy who possibly slept under an overturned dinghy on the beach. He owned a sack and a transistor. He drank Jim Beam mixed with Sprite lemonade. He held long conversations with himself, attempting to provide answers to a series of indignant questions. I would be creeping towards the SIPOs at the water's edge on a low tide, and hear him ask himself in a strangled voice: 'But you never went to her funeral, did you, so what are you talking about?' Poor devil.

The bins made the birds look immense. It's often thought that New Zealand birds are dowdy and down-right boring in appearance, but this is a foolish mistaken notion. Take the SIPOs. They are common enough: the population is estimated at about 85,000, along almost the entire coastal stretch of New Zealand. They breed inland, vast numbers nesting on South Island river beds, and many choose to winter in the warmer northern climates. They are a striking bird, clearly identified by the clean, sharp lines of their black and white plumage, and their vivid red bill. In bright sunlight, the bill — 'remarkably long and remarkably red,' wrote a hero of this book, bird photographer Major Geoffrey Buddle — flames up into a juicy, translucent orange, and so do their eyes.

I kept my distance — it would be despicable to interrupt the vital time wading birds have to feed — when they arrived on the tide shuffling out. The SIPOs inched the shoreline from east to west. They stabbed at bivalves, turning their heads sideways and often under the shallow water as their bill prised open the shells. Not, by the way, of oysters. Buddle: 'If you ask me why "oyster-catcher", I must confess that I do not know. I have never seen one catch an oyster nor attempt to; anyway, I doubt very much if it could it would, or for that matter would if it could, for the simple reason that crabs, shrimps, sand hoppers, and so on are available in plenty just for the taking. However, oyster-catcher it is and has long been all the world over, and there is nothing we can do about it.'

It may or may not be a shame that Buddle fails to provide salacious ruminations on why a shag is called a shag. Officially, they are called cormorants, and I have talked to New Zealand ornithologists who are strict about only ever using that term. Perhaps they dislike the fact its popular name shares the word we use for one of our most popular activities. However, shag it is, and there is nothing we ought to do about it. Like the oystercatcher, the shag is a common sight around New Zealand shores: everyone is familiar with its dramatic pose, that gesture of mercy, when it spreads its wings wide apart to dry after underwater fishing.

Down at my local bay, the SIPOs and the shags filled my bins for many happy hours. So did the New Zealand kingfishers, when they sat immobile on exposed rocks on the shore, and in the overhanging branches of pohutakawa. They waited like that to fly off at incredible speeds in a direct line at their prey, which they caught and then smashed to appalling bloody pieces against a branch. I watched one do this for many happy minutes to a mouse. It stoved its head in. Such violence, and yet the kingfisher has the most peaceful and musical of Latin classifications, *Halcyon sancta*.

Then there were the pair of white-faced heron. In the years I lived beside a mangrove creek I had adored their yellow-toed stealth and graceful flight. Now, at the bay, I spied on their feeding at the water's edge, and in rock pools. Craftily, they rake up the mud floor with one foot, and then pounce on anything desirable that moves. At high tide, I followed the herons as they flew over the bay, across the road, and into a stand of pine trees. They had built a shaggy nest in the crook of high branches. I liked to watch them there towards dusk. As the light dimmed, the trees and the herons lost their texture and became black shapes, a silhouette, an outline. The birds became creatures made of wood. Wood that made a noise: as one bird settled into the nest, the other would pace along nearby branches, and both would set up a long bout of possibly affectionate croaking.

The herons, kingfishers, oystercatchers and good shags were just in the one bay. There are over 200 regular species of bird in New Zealand, urban and rural, at sea and on shore, a swirling presence, yours for the viewing.

Grey Noddy,
Curtis Island,
7.12.06

The trouble
with Walter

WHERE SHOULD YOU be looking, and when? And what are you actually looking for, and looking at? Once again, you need to borrow someone else's eyes. Beginners and experts alike need a field guide. A guide is a bird-watcher's second best friend. There are a few titles available, but you want the best, and the best is *The Field Guide to the Birds of New Zealand* by authors Barrie Heather and Hugh Robertson, and illustrator Derek Onley. You should buy it at once. It's the bible, the greatest book of all time at this precise bird-watching moment in New Zealand.

Even so, I freely admit a great liking for its predecessor, the 1966 guide by Bob Falla, Dick Sibson and Graham Turbott. It contains what is almost certainly the most gothic sentence in New Zealand ornithological literature: 'In 1874 the skin of a freshly dead Australian Darter was found nailed up inside an old shed in Hokitika.'

Before the 1966 guide there was W.R.B. Oliver's landmark 1930 reference volume *New Zealand Birds*, revised in 1955. And before that there was Pérrine Moncrieff's somewhat eccentric but vastly popular *New Zealand Birds and How to Identify Them*, published in 1925. And before that there was the 1904 guide, *The Animals of New Zealand*, which is actually almost entirely about birds, co-authored by Captain Frederick Hutton and that stern, emotional Victorian ornithologist James Drummond.

I couldn't resist. I got the lot, scored in second-hand bookstores, and kept adding. My current bird bibliography weighs in at 37 titles. In part, it was a pursuit of knowledge. Really, though, it was the excitement and greed of discovering a genre of New Zealand writing, a whole new sort of author, a new literature. Inevitably, this led to the one author with whom all New Zealand ornithologists have to deal, have to come to some kind of arrangement. His book is the only real international classic in New Zealand ornithology; his name is like a haunting, the way it bangs and crashes through the ages — that vilified collector of bird skins, Sir Walter Buller.

There is no way you can sidestep Buller's dark shadow. He was born in the Hokianga in 1838, the son of a Wesleyan missionary. His great published work was *A History of the Birds of New Zealand*. There were two editions, published in 1873 and 1888. Graham Turbott edited a very handsome edition in 1967; I found a second-hand copy for $150. The original editions cost $7000. In US currency.

In late 2006, I got my hands on the 1888 edition, fetched up from the storeroom of one of the world's great libraries. It's quite something. The artwork, by Johann Keulmans, is luscious, and usually accurate; Buller's field notes on the birds are evidence of close and passionate observation. Or, as Turbott says in the introduction to his 1967 edition, 'He writes as a naturalist, with keen enjoyment of wild nature and with the naturalist's sure vision.' It's a detailed record of a time and a place, the building of Britain's far-flung colony, set at a crucial point for native birds as they coped — or didn't cope — with a reshaped land suddenly crawling with predators such as rats, stoats and pigs, and drastically altered by farms and towns. In short, it's a priceless historical document — well, yours for only US$7000.

It's also the most violent book about New Zealand birds ever written. Its pages shake with gunshot. Someone has probably compiled a count of how many birds Buller freely admits to killing. There was the white heron: 'In the summer of 1859 (after stalking him for two hours) I shot a beautiful adult male.' Most notoriously, there were his blithely told encounters with huia: 'He came bounding along, and presented himself at close range. This gave me an opportunity of watching this beautiful bird and marking his noble expression, if I may so express it, before I shot him.' And, describing an 1883 trip: 'A pair of Huias, without uttering a sound, appeared in a tree overhead, and as they were caressing each other with their beautiful bills, a charge of No 6 brought both to the ground together.'

The prosecution rests. The huia is now extinct, and Buller is popularly regarded as the bastard who blasted that remarkable forest bird to an early grave. Naturally, he was cast as a whiskered Victorian villain in Nick Drake's biographical play *Dr Buller's Birds*, performed at Circa Theatre, Wellington in 2006. Buller has 'the blood of the last huia on his hands'. He is facing 'the dark night of the soul'. He contemplates his sins, his wrongful intervention in the sacred 'Maori ecology of the land'. What pantomime. What dreary, simple-minded nonsense.

In reality Buller was a complex case. God knows how many huia he took down, but the bird's fate was decided more by the introduction of predators and the felling of native forest. Buller actually urged the government to establish island sanctuaries for the bird. In 1892 he successfully lobbied for it to be given protected status. And yet the next year he went into the bush and grabbed more specimens for his clients. 'I was appalled to discover what Buller had done,' his biographer Ross Galbreath told science writer Rebecca Priestley. 'He was a real rascal in some ways.'

In some ways... Bird collecting was an established practice in Buller's era; the question is how far he took it. The cantankerous, gifted naturalist Brian Parkinson has argued that other collectors of the time were more responsible than Buller, although Buller tuts about the 'zeal' of his contemporaries, and also dobs in Maori, referring to a party of eleven who hunted huia for a month in the Manawatu Gorge and came back with 646 skins.

In the preface to his 1888 edition, he writes, 'It has been the author's desire to collect and place on record a complete life history of these birds before their extirpation should have rendered such a task impossible.' The previous year, the British naturalist Professor Newton had given an address in Manchester, where he said, 'I am told by Sir Walter Buller that in New Zealand one may now live for weeks and months without seeing a single example of its indigenous birds.'

At worst, this reads like a kind of wishful thinking: Buller shared the risible nineteenth-century notion that Maori, too, were a dying race. In an 1885 speech he said that 'in all probability, five and twenty years hence there will only be a remnant [of Maori] left.' The task of civilised Europeans, Buller thought, was to preserve these last traces − 'to smooth down their dying pillow'. What odious words.

If he thought the same of our birds, you have to assume his idea of a nice pillow was the Zoological Society's Gardens in Regents Park, London, to which he dispatched two huia. (It's possible Keulemans visited here when he made his illustrative studies for Buller's books.) Incredible to think of the female huia in the London parrot house, between a toucan and a hornbill, fed boiled eggs, fresh meat and worms. Its fate? Buller: 'It died in a much emaciated condition.'

Better to have shot it. Truly. Without Buller and his ilk, no physical record might exist of birds that were headed for a fall. I asked Brian Gill, the softly spoken and eminently sensible curator of birds at the Auckland Museum, whether we are in debt to the shotgun politics of collectors. He said, 'That legacy in terms of reaching the public, inspiring by way of education – what a valuable thing it's been.'

The museum has 13,000 bird skins; Te Papa and the Canterbury Museum each have about 20,000. These days, the majority of fresh skins come from dead birds picked up on beach patrols. Would it be good to have more collecting of perfect specimens in the field? 'In some cases it might be,' Gill said. 'A classic situation would be the rock wren. New Zealand wrens are incredibly important birds. The latest DNA work is showing that they are the sister group to all the other passerines, the perching birds, which are a huge group of birds, and the first branch of their evolutionary tree were the New Zealand wrens.

They're the most primitive survivors. They are incredibly important ornithologically; they're like living fossils. The rock wren is very rare and probably declining. There are almost no specimens left in our collection. Museums asked for permission to collect them and were turned down. I think that's short-sighted.'

Hurry now while stocks last. With the huia, Buller charged in when he could – and even after he couldn't – once bagging 16 in a single shooting spree. What an exquisite bird it was, about the size of a magpie, black with a shiny green gloss, its bill ivory white, a rich orange wattle adorning the female. It hopped, bounding along forest floors in the Ruahine, Tararua and Rimutaka ranges. Its astonishing feature was the weird and very rare nature of its sexual dimorphism; Sir Richard Owen, when he first studied the remains of a male and female huia, thought they were two completely different species. The sexes of most birds look exactly the same, but the huia went right out there, the male short-billed, the female with its bill curved in a long, elegant parabola. Exquisite, and dead and buried, the last definite report in 1907, although unconfirmed sightings have been as agonisingly recent as 1960.

Buller thought that hunting had once caused a decline in population. He was right. In 1888, though, he claimed, 'The bird is now far more plentiful.' He remains the wrongest person in the history of New Zealand birds.

Heron
(blue, white-faced)

A visitor from Australia

THE PESTILENCE OF rat and possum, the years of slash and burn, and the Buller years of cultural imperialism gave the birdland of New Zealand a sound thrashing. Recovery has been slow. There are still far too many endangered species, and bird-watchers need to maintain an eternal vigilance against the threat of environmental damage. But the worst years of bust are over. New Zealand is now enjoying the boom years. It may not last – declining populations of some birds offer depressing truth about global warming – but New Zealanders are holding onto birds for dear life.

Eradication programmes of predators such as the possum and the rat are proving effective. The regeneration of native bush is proving effective. And inland bird sanctuaries in Karori, Waitakere, Mount Bruce and most recently Maungatautari Mountain, as well as the island sanctuaries on Tiritiri Matangi, Kapiti and Motuara, are proving spectacularly effective. In 2006, a member of parliament, Marian Hobbs, threatened to quit the government when the Cabinet rejected an ambitious six-million-dollar bid by the Karori sanctuary to provide a visitors' centre. Hobbs had lobbied hard for the cash: 'You can't imagine how hurt I feel having fought this through. It's embarrassing. It's bloody hurtful.' If she had made good her threat, the possible loss of her Wellington electorate would have seriously damaged Labour's fragile alliance. A government for a stitchbird.

Offshore, a previously unknown population of snipe have appeared on Campbell Island in the subantarctic; in towns and cities, native birds such as the tui are more abundant. It's led to a growing and overt love affair that New Zealanders are feeling towards their own birds.

In 2005, the tui won a Royal Forest and Bird public poll as New Zealand's favourite bird. The following year, the total number of votes tripled. This time the winner was the fantail. In both years, the top ten were a who's who of native species – our emblematic birds, almost all birds of the bush, the exalted K club of kiwi, kakapo, kokako, kea, kereru (New Zealand pigeon) and korimako (bellbird). Expect the kaka to feature in next year's list — urban sightings of that large antique parrot are becoming frequent.

All well and good, except that it's inspired that reflex kick that is always itching for release: nationalism. Native birds — the K club, and the tui, fantail and a few other obvious candidates — are seen as the only birds that truly count. Hence, almost the only time we hear about birds in New Zealand is when they're under threat. While the conservation movement utters a long lament, how often do we hear about bird populations that are doing real well, thanks, and that it's due to human populations?

Take the kingfisher. It's flourished in urban New Zealand: lots of introduced mice are just dying to have their heads stoved in, and power lines and posts provide excellent viewing platforms above the killing fields. Actually, the kingfisher was once thought to have adapted *too* well. Buller notes: 'In Wanganui it provoked the hostility of the Acclimatisation Society by preying on the young of the House sparrow, which had been introduced at great expense; and the committee encouraged a crusade against the offendors by offering a premium on kingfishers' heads.'

That bizarre story also serves as a reminder of the role played by acclimatisation societies in the array of birds we now take for granted. Filled with longing, and probably wanting to smother New Zealand native birds

with a pillow, nineteenth-century British settlers filled
the skies with birds from 'Home'. House sparrows were
introduced in 1865 – by Buller: 'I must plead guilty to
having been accessory to their importation, having
advertised in the London papers offering a reward of 100
pounds for 100 pairs delivered alive in the colony.'

Starlings arrived in 1862–63, thrushes in 1862–78,
blackbirds in 1862–75, mynas in 1870–77. There were
also liberations of four kinds of finches (chaffinch,
greenfinch, goldfinch, redpoll) and, from Australia,
over 1000 magpies. A few species didn't take; there
were, for example, unsuccessful attempts to bring in the
nightingale and English robin.

It might be instructive if the grandly named Royal
Forest and Bird Protection Society held a poll to deter-
mine the public's *least* favourite birds. In the pecking
order of New Zealand's bird species, the English birds –
common as muck, all over the shop – would rate scarcely
above the bottom rung, down there with the rock pigeon,
that cooing nincompoop of the city, and the unjustly
despised gulls and Australian magpie. But the English
birds deserve respect, and admiration. Study of their
characteristics and behaviour are just as fulfilling as
those of any other bird. Almost certainly the most violent
paper ever published in *Notornis*, the Ornithological
Society journal, is 'Nature Red in Claw: How and Why
Starlings Kill Each Other', the result of a 20-year nest-
box study, written by J. E. C. and M. M. Flux, in 1992,

complete with graphic photographs of two birds with their claws dug deep into each other's murdered head.

Good luck to the native birds cowering in the bush. But most of us live at home. The birds around us are brilliant to watch, to observe, to get to know. That most definitely includes the introduced English birds. Example: every now and then during spring, blackbirds decide to attack car mirrors, because they regard their reflection as some new intruder. The show also includes birds that have arrived under their own steam, often from Australia. One of the great appeals of watching birds is the constant change. Birds exit, birds arrive. Birds don't sit still; they migrate, they turn up in places no one ever anticipates. Places like New Zealand.

Australia has given us birds such as the silvereye in 1865, and the spur-winged plover in 1932: the manager of a borstal farm in Southland alerted bird-watcher Very Reverend C.J. Tocker to a pair of 'strange birds'. Later, Maida Barlow of Invercargill made plovers her specialist study, recording the oldest bird in New Zealand (it was 16) and writing a minor classic, *The Year of the Spur-winged Plover*.

Another visitor from Australia set up shop during the war. 'Rare in New Zealand,' writes Moncrieff in 1925, about the white-faced heron. 'There is no record of the nests of this species having been found in New Zealand,' writes Oliver in 1930. The birds began breeding in New Zealand as recently as 1941, at Shag River in Otago.

They are now so widespread, a familiar sight on shores, farms and rugby fields, that it's strange to imagine a New Zealand without their yellow-toed footprints, without the opportunity to gaze through bins at their lovely plumage of pink turning to grey turning to soft, delicate blue, at the way they croak to each other at dusk, staying close to the nest, protecting a new life.

Tui,
Little Barrier

The tribe

A VERY GREAT SIN was committed in the previous chapter, and that was to refer to 'birdwatchers'. That term just won't do. It's nothing short of an insult to people who know about birds. The correct term is birders. English author Mark Cocker sorts that out very early on in his hilarious social history, *Birders: Tales of a Tribe*, published in 2001. What birders do, he explains through gritted teeth, is called birding. It's active. It travels vast distances, it takes careful notes, it does things on behalf of birds. What birders don't do, he adds with heavy emphasis, is indulge in mere bird-watching.

He's right. Bird-watching is all very well, it doesn't do anyone any harm, but it's passive. It's dozy, indolent. Those content days of autumn and winter at my local bay, armed with sandwiches and cigarettes, quietly picking my way over mud as falling leaves twitched in the sunlight, and smoke rose on the opposite shore from the Chelsea sugar factory – that was bird-watching.

The trouble is that bird-watching is my speed. I lead a dozy, indolent life. I don't drive; I can go a week without discovering the world beyond the corner dairy. My local bay was even closer than the dairy. If it had stocked cigarettes I would have been the happiest man alive. A few minutes' trot was all it took to lose myself among the wading birds while the homeless drunk lost himself in Jim Beam and Sprite. And all I did was watch the birds, because I like bird-watching. It's such an easy pleasure. It doesn't require hard work. It's perfectly innocent, even though you can sometimes cut a low, suspicious figure wandering around with a pair of binoculars.

You don't really even have to leave home. Wild birdseed, sold at supermarkets, is a cheap and guaranteed way to attract birds – the passerines, or perching birds, such as the house sparrow and starling, as well as silvereyes and a variety of colourful finches – to your house. Even better, the tui, bellbird, Barbary dove, and spotted dove are increasingly regular garden visitors, depending on where you live. Plant with birds in mind – tree fuchsia and kowhai for the honey-eating bellbird and tui, for instance. You could go the whole hog and knock up a bird box, and whatever happened to bird baths?

This kind of bird-watching appeals to the nana within all of us. It's so... domestic. A very clear line separates bird-watchers from birders, who apply strenuous thought and methods to what is much more than a nice pastime. As such, I was terrified when I first started attending meetings of the official body of New Zealand birders – the Ornithological Society, or OS.

There is a stock image of ornithologists. It's courtesy of the one film maker who is more famous for birds than even David Attenborough: Alfred Hitchcock. His classic film *The Birds* gave a fear and loathing of not just wild birds to the modern subconscious. The film's resident bird expert, Mrs Bundy, turns up in the town's cafe just before the birds run amok and imperiously announces, 'Ornithology happens to be my vocation.' She then throws out a few learned remarks about moulting and flocking. But for all her knowledge, she has no idea what's happening. With her beret and mannish bearing, she's cast as an old bat, bad news, an eccentric fool. 'Birds are not aggressive creatures,' she claims. The cook interrupts her with an order: 'Three Southern fried chicken, Sam!' When she scoffs at warnings that the birds are about to attack, she's put in her place with a devastating put-down: 'Mrs Bundy, why don't you go home and polish your binoculars?' The last we see of the film's ornithologist she is cowering, traumatised and ashamed, after the birds have reduced the town to ashes.

I got talking to a nice old dear one night at the monthly meeting of the South Auckland OS branch. It was her first time too. She had actually come the previous month, but as she had stood outside looking at the birders inside the brightly lit shed of the Papakura Croquet Club, she had had an attack of shyness, and turned and fled. I knew exactly how she felt. During a break, I went outside for a cigarette, and stood in the chill night air, looking in through the window at the gathering of about 20 birders. They bustled about with their knowledge and their commitment, confidently discussing copulation, and were more intimidating than the other hobbyists who had gathered that night in a hall on the other side of the bowling green for a class in kickboxing. I never saw the nice old dear again.

But there was nothing to be frightened of. The birders were funny and welcoming, a happy bunch of middle New Zealanders, with their beards and their jerseys and their arcane dialogue. Members of OS routinely see novices arrive in their midst; they can usually tell straight off if newcomers have the right stuff, the true calling.

Among themselves, there was a fair amount of bickering, jealousy, and territorial squabblings: the usual office politics, made stranger by the fact they didn't have an office. But they were governed by an ethic of utter selflessness – they were in it for and on behalf of the birds, and worked tirelessly, adventurously, merrily, towards that end. They could sometimes, though, be killjoys, wringing their hands about the threat posed to birds by people having fun — in particular, kite-surfing, and walking dogs on beaches. One person asked, 'Could there be warnings put on cans of dog food?' Leisure didn't seem part of their vocabulary. They went to work, bending their heads and backs to the task of bird study, and their attitude was: all hands on deck.

They were very white: you could count the number of Maori birders on one claw. They were very English: eight of the OS regional representatives came from England. This figure was pointed out to me by an OS regional representative who came from England. He said, 'It's the same in Australia. We had a bunch of Australians come here to look at the storm petrel. Of the party of eleven, one was Canadian, nine were Brits, and one spoke with an Australian accent.'

England is the home of birding. As I was to discover later on a trek through Norfolk and East Anglia, it strikes the population like a disease. It has its own culture, its own customs, including that famous English characteristic of forming an orderly, disgruntled queue wherever possible. The harsh light of New Zealand softens the English. It was hard to tell the English members of OS from the locals. Almost everyone in the society I met was marked by an easy New Zealandness — they were casual, open, friendly, smart, mocking, self-mocking.

They had chosen — or were drawn to, without asking why — a subject of inexhaustible interest. There is no end-game in the pursuit of knowledge about birds. Once in, you're in for life.

In 2006, membership of the OS nationally stood at 919. As well as the monthly meetings, where notes and observations are shared, and a guest is introduced to give A Most Interesting Talk, members contribute to core activities — bird-banding, wader counts, bird distribution, constant monitoring of migratory habits, and beach patrols to count and sometimes collect dead birds. There are field trips, and members receive *Notornis*, which over the years has featured such classics as 'An attempt to restore sex to the Cape Pigeon', 'What do keas die of?' and 'The mineral content of the faeces of the pukeko'. And there are usually doomed attempts to get schools interested. One idea floated in 2006 was to popularise the five-minute bird count, in which you count the variety and number of birds in one spot for five minutes every day for weeks, months, maybe a year. It's a worthwhile practice, internationally recognised, but how many schoolkids can stay still for five minutes?

OS was formed in 1940. In 2007 it will change its name to Birding New Zealand. The new title brings it into line with its colleagues across the Tasman, Birding Australia, but it's something of a sad loss. 'Ornithological Society' has a seriousness of intent, advertises its special expertise. Still, it could have been worse: it could have adopted the gross modern habit of affixing a 'z' to its name, as in Birdenz.

I'm glad I joined when it was still called OS. It felt like signing up to an élite, a crack force, with its proud tradition and attitude of scholarship. Of course, I was way out of my depth. I came armed with only a bare outline of bird evolution ('Dinosaurs did not become extinct,' said David Attenborough. 'They only flew away.') And although I swotted up on issues of *Notornis* and even a 1966 biology text for sixth-form students ('Of all modern reptiles, crocodiles show the closest anatomical affinities to birds'), and learned that birds maintain a constant internal temperature, alter the pitch of their song by two pairs of muscles somewhere near the trachea, and the turkey scores 93 heartbeats per minute while the house sparrow bangs away at 460, I still found it difficult to identify birds in flight, couldn't tell a male from a female, and the helpful descriptions of bird calls in the *Field Guide* ('Call of the New Zealand Robin is a soft "chirp"') were of no help whatsoever.

Birders talk about how each bird has its own special life force, its own 'jizz'. I never saw any evidence of jizz. I retreated from the air to the dark rooms of the imagination. I started dreaming about birds, and hallucinated that I saw birds in words. There was the day I walked along a city street, stopped in my tracks, and turned back to look at what I thought was a really striking sticker about birds on a car window: MIGRANT OF FITNESS. But all it said was WARRANT OF FITNESS.

As someone who writes for a living, and who probably spends more time writing than living, I was more at home in the swirling presence of words than the swirling presence of birds. I curled up with my library of New Zealand bird books. The older the better. These early authors were pioneering something important, something significant; it was exciting to watch our lazy sensual isles at the end of the world take shape through their eyes. As much as I learned from the living OS tribe, I was transported by the dead authors – the tribal elders.

Pied Oystercatcher
nests on the sand,
Pakiri, 28.12.39

Serbian eagle

NEW ZEALAND'S most famous tribal elder of birds is Herbert Guthrie-Smith. His 1921 book *Tutira*, a natural history of his Hawke's Bay sheep station, remains a classic of New Zealand writing, routinely featuring in lists of the best ten or 20 books. But Guthrie-Smith also wrote three books devoted exclusively to birds – *Birds of the Water, Wood and Waste* (1908), *Mutton Birds and Other Birds* (1914), and *Bird Life on Island and Shore* (1925). These little masterpieces overflow with wonder and despair at native birds: his final book, published in 1936, was called *The Joys and Sorrows of a New Zealand Naturalist.*

A biography of Nelson woman Pérrine Moncrieff (1893–1979) is in the works. About time. She wore a cap of white hens' feathers dyed sapphire blue, kept a pet macaw called Miss Macawber, and was crucial in the establishment of Abel Tasman National Park in 1942. I spoke to a few people who knew her; they all used exactly the same word: 'formidable'. She was outspoken, determined. She wasn't popular. She became a Wildlife Service ranger in 1947, after the department had rejected her on the basis of gender in the 1930s, when she first applied. According to environmental researcher Robin Hodge, she 'especially wanted to chase up poachers of kereru, godwits and other protected birds.'

As the author of the nifty and best-selling field guide *New Zealand Birds and How to Identify Them*, Moncrieff was the most high-profile woman ornithologist in New Zealand, when the discipline was – still is, mostly – led by men. As such, writes Hodge, Moncrieff was often reduced to a figure of fun; bird blokes joked about her with lines such as, 'Come up and see my Tits.'

But she was hardly an outcast. Pérrine and her husband Malcolm Moncrieff were fabulously wealthy. They had servants. Their home shuddered with antiques. As in England in the first half of the nineteenth century, the study of birds in New Zealand was largely confined to the rich. They could afford the time. They were country gents, with English money and C of E credentials, people like Reverend Thomas Henry Potts (1824–88), who ran the massive South Island sheep station Hakatere, and authored *Out in the Open*, a lovingly composed, attentive book about native birds. He arrived from England in 1851 after making his fortune as an arms manufacturer, although back then they were called gun makers.

Almost all of New Zealand's truly admired early ornithologists have been awarded an obituary in *Notornis*. Guthrie-Smith, Moncrieff, W. R. B. Oliver, Charles Fleming, Robert Falla, Bob Stidolph, Dick Sibson, the Wilkinsons of Kapiti Island, Peter Bull, Captain John Jenkins, Count Kazimierz Antoni z Granowa Wodzicki ... it can read like a book of the dead. The greatest obituary, the best written, composed with feeling and appreciation, was by Major Robert Wilson of Edgar Stead. It begins: 'Edgar Stead is dead.' Wilson and Stead had shared a remarkable friendship with another man, Major Geoffrey Buddle, and the story of these three birdwatchers is something that could only have happened in these islands.

Each man wrote one book. Stead's *The Life Histories of New Zealand Birds* (1932), Buddle's *Bird Secrets* (1951) and Wilson's *Bird Islands of New Zealand* (1959) are all beautifully produced volumes, relics of another age. All three men were monied, men of leisure, and absolutely dedicated in the pursuit of knowledge of New Zealand birds. Together, in pairs or the three of them, they travelled the country, often to remote offshore islands, on bird study expeditions; how strange to think of them charging around some of the most obscure corners of New Zealand to look at birds at a time when all the anxious intellectual blather was about finding a 'national identity'. They found it in the air, and had tremendous fun doing it.

They were also very good shots, especially Stead. He ordered 50,000 shotgun cartridges every year from England until his death in 1949. It's doubtful he wasted much ammunition. Once, in Raetihi, he flushed then shot 16 quail without a miss, with rights and lefts, sometimes taking the right barrel one side of a manuka bush and the left barrel the other side. The gentleman naturalist with a smoking gun: as further evidence of his station in life, he served as president of the Christchurch bridge club, and was a world authority on rhododendrons.

Major Wilson allows that his close friend could be 'overbearing'. Stead's book takes Buller to task (correctly) on a point of shag behaviour, and lambasts 'irresponsible hoodlums' who shot terns and gulls at the mouth of the Rakaia in the early 1900s. As well, it's a marvellous record of 18 bird species, and Stead was a good photographer of birds, too – the best is his amazing shot of a 'slaughter yard', showing the remains of over 150 mottled petrels, butchered by those homicidal sea birds, the southern skua.

Life in New Zealand is given to eccentricities. At first glance, it seems supremely eccentric that two army majors – Buddle of Auckland and Wilson of Bulls –

were at the forefront of New Zealand ornithology, but there was depth and sadness to their calling. The two galloping majors were both awarded the Distinguished Service Order in World War I. Wilson served in the Royal Garrison Artillery, and was transferred to the New Zealand Expeditionary Force; he was wounded in 1918, and later shipped back home, to Bulls. A photograph of Wilson in full military dress shows him staring out from a pair of firm, steady eyes. He looks like a tough nut. Buddle's photograph captures a sensitivity, but he was undoubtedly brave. He lived through the hell of Gallipoli. His DSO was awarded for bridge-building under fire, and he also won the Military Cross.

Educated at Auckland Grammar, Buddle was seriously gassed in France and not expected to live. He was packed off to a sanatorium in Scotland. That didn't take, and he journeyed back as an invalid to New Zealand. He stopped over in Suva, where his health picked up with rest and a lot of sunbathing. Further treatment came as a patient at the old TB hospital in Cambridge.

Were birds the final cure? There seemed something precious, even life-saving, about that bond. I heard mention of a brief, unhappy marriage in Scotland. Later, back in New Zealand, he fell in love, but the woman's father made marriage impossible. I thought of Buddle on his bird expeditions with his married friends Stead and Wilson, and was once again reminded of Matthew

Arnold's line about birds: 'Beside us, but alone.' I doubt I am imagining that Buddle's photographs in his book *Bird Secrets* have a strange beauty to them, a peculiar peacefulness.

Wilson's *Bird Islands of New Zealand* is the saddest book ever written in New Zealand ornithological literature. From his introduction: 'It has been written in memory of my two companions on these island trips, Edgar Stead and Major Geoffrey Buddle, DSO, MC, Serbian Eagle.' Of his relationship with the two men, he self-effaces: 'In both cases I was the henchman.' He adds: 'Since their deaths I have reluctantly ceased my bird trips.'

This elegiac tone continues throughout the book, an evocative account of expeditions to islands including the Poor Knights, Hen and Chickens, Stewart, and the various Muttonbird islands. Wilson's chief subject is sea birds – the petrels, shearwaters and prions. He has such an inquiring mind, such a good pair of eyes and ears. It's first-class fieldwork, and some of the best travel writing about New Zealand you'll ever read.

What a singular book. Birds, everywhere; but in the background, quiet, constant, a warm presence, are the figures of Stead and Buddle. Their 'henchman' has written a love story.

Young Morepork,
Great King, 2.12.45

An old
rooster

S TEAD, BUDDLE, WILSON: I
was too late for these legends, they
had flown the coop, but I took a cab
on a warm afternoon in March to
snare a living legend in his Titirangi nest. Everyone in
New Zealand ornithology knows of Geoff Moon. He is
very likely the best bird photographer this country has
ever produced. I already owned a copy of his first book,
the stunning *Focus on New Zealand Birds*, published in
1957. When I noticed in the bookstores a new book under
his name, with the rather familiar title *New Zealand
Birds in Focus*, I figured it was perhaps his son. It couldn't
be the same bloke, I reasoned. Not after 50 years. But the

author of 2006 was the one and the same author of 1957, now a slender, quite hilarious old rooster who was about to turn 91.

His laugh was a loud and immensely cheerful hoot: 'Hah!' He had a very generous head of hair. His eyes were sharp. He migrated from England in 1947; his mating habits have produced four children; he said, 'I love the sea. And plants. And the bush. And insects...'

Above all, he loved birds. You could see that at a glance in his photographs, and you could also detect a keen knowledge and understanding of birds. He said, 'I'm not so much interested in photographing birds just for a portrait. I'm interested in bird behaviour. That's why I spend a lot of time in hides not taking photographs, just taking notes. I actually don't like being labelled a bird photographer. I'm a naturalist at heart.'

Of all his books, perhaps his masterpiece is the sumptuous *Birds Around Us* (1979). He took a quiet pride in his work, but what moved him was the subject. Moon knew that other New Zealand, a particular geography where borders and centres were defined by birds. When you looked at the photographs, you felt the photographer's pleasure – red-crested parakeets inside a hole in a pohutakawa tree overhanging a cliff on Hen Island, welcome swallows flying to a nest under a road bridge near Hikurangi, reef herons in a cave on an islet near Kawau Island, crested grebes in a nest of sticks and waterweeds on Lake Alexandra.

He did an awful lot more than take pictures. Moon's field notes were a significant influence on the 1966 *Field Guide*. In more recent years, OS members have vigorously lobbied for him to be elected a Life Fellow of the society. They are right to resent the fact that their applications have so far been rejected.

Moon's greatest work has been on moreporks and kingfishers. He captured the first photograph of a diving kingfisher showing that a protective membrane closes over its eye just as it touches water. He devoted countless hours to spying on the morepork. When it flew he heard nothing, but felt a wind on his face: 'The wings of a morepork have this velvety edge to the flight feathers, so they fly absolutely silently.' Once, high up in a tree at some ungodly hour waiting to get eye to eye with that night owl, he electrocuted himself on a 2500-volt charge while changing a flash bulb, 'felt a sensation of being inflated', and was knocked unconscious. 'Lucky I didn't fall off and kill myself,' he said. 'Hah! Oh dear.'

It was rather startling when Moon pointed to a book by the acclaimed British nature photographer Heather Angel and said, 'She's a real goer.' But this was his highest form of praise. He meant she got out there, investigated, did the work.

He's that same kind of active bird, or was – it had been two years since he last lurked inside one of his famous home-made wooden hides in the New Zealand bush. 'It is a wonderful experience being in a hide,' he said, with real longing. So much of his life has passed in one of these contraptions: 'I got up to Mark 7b.' Built from light timber frames, covered with either canvas or a sheet of calico painted to stiffen them against a breeze, the hides went with him all over New Zealand. You can see them neatly folded on the roof of his Cortina in a photo taken sometime in the 1970s in his latest book. The car is stuck in shingle near Lake Ellesmere. Moon is jacking the car up. He looks the happiest man alive.

On the afternoon I visited, he had the run of the house; his wife Lynette was visiting a grandchild in Malaysia. There were cut flowers in a vase. The carpet seemed freshly vacuumed. Dominating one wall was a framed letter and a drawing of an English dipper, sent to him by the artist Raymond Ching in 1961. I stretched out my legs and was in no hurry to leave. When he said his basement was full of Bolex 16mm films of diving gannets, I shivered with delight at the thought of a basement in Titirangi containing so much life.

I asked about his life. He was born in China. He could trace his ancestry back to a knight who served William the Conqueror. Sent to school in Essex, he explored a fabulous marshland, teeming with things such as voles and poisonous adders. He trained to be a vet, and remembers boiling a dead dog's head on a gas ring. He was sent to the Isle of Wight during the war — the Germans dropped a bomb on a herd of cows. He liked the sound of New Zealand, and ignored a friend who wrote him a six-page letter stating reasons not to come here. He set up practice in Warkworth.

He knew all the leading names in New Zealand ornithology. There was Ken Bigwood, who pioneered bird sound recordings: 'Very difficult man to get on with.' There was the black-backed gull watcher and much else, Graham Turbott, now in a rest-home in Epsom: 'Very nice fellow. Quiet chap.' There was Dr Michael Soper: 'Probably our best photographer of birds. Wasn't an easy guy to get on with.'

Moon had a gentle manner. The way he moved revealed an obvious agility and strength. Above all, there was a curiosity about him, a lively intelligence. He said, 'I hated school. Except for sport. And chemistry. And art. And physics. And geography.' He didn't hate school at all, except for Latin. 'I used to daydream through a boring Latin lesson, and make plans about where I'd go wandering in the marshes. Nature was in my blood right from the start.'

When he was ten, he discovered a sparrowhawk's nest with three chicks in a tree. Inspired by the bird photographer Oliver Pike, he built a hide near the nest. Moon writes in his latest book: 'I entered it soon after dawn … I held my breath when the chicks started to squeak as they saw a parent arriving to feed them. I was transfixed and my heart was pounding as I watched … In spite of the extreme discomfort of sitting in the hide on a leaning branch, I spent several hours there, fascinated by the amazing spectacle I was observing at such close quarters.'

What he wanted was to record the moments. He bought an enormous Thornton-Pickard at a junk stall, but was unable to afford a good lens – until a newspaper bought a photo he took of his aunt's cat eating a cucumber. Preposterous, but he was on his way. The tools of his trade were his bins and his scope, and the TP Reflex and Sanderson field camera, the Asahi Pentax, the Olympus OM-1, the Mamiya RB67, the Nikon F100, the Nikon F4…

I asked him a simple question: how to watch a bird. He had a simple answer. 'Birds have a great sense of hearing. Don't bash through the bush if you want to see them. You see far more if you just take the trouble to sit down. I used to carry a plastic bag so I could sit down on a wet bank. Just sit down, and quietly watch. All sorts of things happen.'

*White-eye feeding
young, Okere,
14.1.38*

An older
rooster

I N THE BEGINNING there was
Graham Turbott. With his deep sense
of modesty, he will doubtless despair
at the suggestion he is godlike, but at
92 Turbott is the grand old man of New Zealand
ornithology. Along with legends such as Stead, Wilson,
and Moncrieff, he was among a select group of only 15
people who formed the Ornithological Society of New
Zealand in 1938.

Turbott is the only one of those originals left standing.
Which he was, quite capably thanks, his long, loping
stride carrying his classic New Zealand male birder's
build – tall, rangy, trim as a tent pole – when I had the

pleasure of visiting him at his retirement apartment on an afternoon in May. He kept a tidy ship. The apartment was immaculate. He had his Pentax 7 X 50 bins on the window ledge. Later, he fished out the birder's other essential tool of the trade — a small waterproof notebook to record his observations. He had literally filled enough notebooks to last a lifetime: Turbott was a birder back when they were called bird-watchers, as a boy growing up in Stanley Bay on Auckland's North Shore, and later as staff zoologist at the Auckland Museum from 1937 to 1957, assistant director of the Canterbury Museum for the next seven years, then back at the Auckland Museum as director for 15 years, until retiring in 1979.

Born in 1914, he was a foundation pupil at Takapuna Grammar in 1927. He took to birds early. He said, 'There are people who take to bird-watching as a pleasure without hesitating. It just needs a bit of sympathetic observing; it's a personal pleasure to identify the bird you're looking at, to develop the habit of accurate observing. When you look at Geoff Moon's photos, you know he's aware of the exact shape and colour and habit of the bird. A little old lady said to me the other day, "There's a bird with yellow on its head out with the sparrows." But it was a goldfinch. It has yellow on its shoulders, not on its head.'

As a child, it was Turbott's fate that he lived down the street from Robert Falla — later Sir Robert Falla — an early authority on New Zealand birds, who would be

Turbott's co-author on the landmark 1966 *Field Guide*. Turbott said, 'I was very lucky. He was terribly good when I was a kid. I remember one day he told me to catch a tram to Greenwood Corner, where he picked me up and we went to Manukau Harbour. We got there, and I remember him saying, "Now, there's a Caspian tern." He said, "Borrow my field glasses." The only tool a bird-watcher needs is something with which to get a closer look. That was the moment I became addicted.'

Turbott's story is the story of New Zealand ornithology. Of course, he bought a copy of Moncrieff's *New Zealand Birds* when it was published in 1925 (he was still at primary school) and then W. R. B. Oliver's volume, in 1930: 'That was a big event.' He met both the authors — he met everyone.

There was Edgar Stead: 'The best shot in the South Island. In a way he was the tail-end of the Buller tradition. Stead was the first recorder of a whole lot of migrants coming to Lake Ellesmere, and he popped them off. I was at the tail-end of it, too... Oh, sure! Any self-respecting bird section of any museum in those days had a gun. I've shot up the odd specimen. I popped off a few fantails from the Three Kings. I've been guilty. But I've never shot a saddleback...'

He explored offshore islands for birds with Major Wilson, as well as Major Buddle, who became a close friend: 'I knew him as Bud. He was a marvellous chap. He was obviously a brave man — DSO was the highest honour next to the VC. He'd been badly gassed, and could walk only a short distance without panting. I've been so lucky in going to places that are really primitive New Zealand – the Hen and Chickens, Little Barrier, Poor Knights. These are unaltered places, and Bud and I did as much of that as we could. He lived under Mount Hobson and drove an early model car. I went to the Poor Knights with both the majors. They were very strict about camp discipline, but they were both such good fun.'

Turbott had such knowledge, such experience; it seemed a dreadful oversight he had not been made Sir Graham. He even served his country, as they say. One of the very strangest chapters in New Zealand ornithology is known as the 'Cape Expedition' – a totally hush-hush operation, in which Turbott and a band of colleagues were sent by the government to perform coast-watching duties on the subantarctic Auckland Islands during World War II. 'Cape Expedition' was the code name. Turbott's year-long tour of duty began on 20 December 1943, sailing into Ranui Cove on the *New Golden Hind*, a luxury 91-foot yacht built by a wealthy Auckland businessman.

The men were issued with full army kit, but dressed as civilians. If captured, they were to say they were fishermen. Their job? To keep an eye on enemy shipping. They didn't see any. There wasn't any. But in between his daily inspections of the flat, undisturbed horizon at

6 a.m., midday and 6 p.m., Turbott kept himself busy. He read *War and Peace*, three times over, and took advantage of that rare opportunity to take detailed notes of sea birds such as the Arctic tern and the southern skua.

Island life was cold, it was barren, it was strictly for the birds. Turbott enjoyed that year just fine. Very little seemed to perturb him. He was a lovely man, kind and considerate, and he had a very sly sense of humour. Also, and this is a quality that really only few old people possess, he was wise. There was something about him – maybe it was his sense of equilibrium.

I asked him about the birds of his childhood, and he staggered me by quoting from one of my columns in *Sunday* magazine. I'd written: 'Bravo to the protected species huddling on sanctuaries and islands. But most of us live at home ... I am in love with the birds around us.' Turbott said, 'You made an important point – "most of us live at home". We don't go to Little Barrier or Fiordland and so on. The birds we have in New Zealand are partly the introduced species, and partly the natives. The natives are very much divided into those that adapted and live all around us, and those that took a bombshell after colonisation.

'The answer to your question is that in our Stanley Bay garden we had blackbirds, thrushes, silvereyes, finches, fantail, grey warbler, and kingfisher. They were the birds all around us. And they're marvellous birds. I'm all for blackbirds. Most successful bird in the world, really.

Ecologically, it's perhaps the most important. It's everywhere: it's the one that's eating the insect pests in the garden, and the fields. In its own right it's a handsome bird, and that's partly why I was keen to go to Oxford — in my earlier days, the British Council offered me a trip for six months to the Edward Grey Institute of Field Ornithology — to see what the British made of their own birds.

'It varies in New Zealand as to which birds have survived under which circumstances. Some native birds have penetrated into the exotic forests — whitehead and robin are common. We have a give and take going on. The whole thing's a dynamic, because we're getting birds from Australia — the spur-winged plover, the swallow.'

I mentioned to him that he had seen only the second recorded welcome swallow in New Zealand, in 1941 on the Cape Expedition. He said, 'A lot of species are new since I was a boy. And yet kingfishers were already revelling in the colonial landscape. As Edgar Stead quite rightly said, "The coming of telephone wires was heaven for kingfishers." He even drew the difference between copper-drawn wires and steel wires, as to which the kingfisher liked best.

'That's been one of my main interests, the situation as the landscape changes. New Zealanders could do with being more relaxed in the settled landscape, which is what you were getting at in your article. There's a growing tendency to discount any interest in anything

other than the rare native birds. I don't know whether
it's a Calvinistic reaction against the sins of our grand-
parents, but it's as if you're not allowed to speak about
anything except a kakapo or a saddleback.

'That's getting a bit extreme. I suppose a lot of the
Department of Conservation staff's bread and butter
depends on working on them. Well, fine. I would spend
money on saving the last kakapo. It's immensely
demanding; Don Merton is showing what can be done
with saving the black robin. We're famous all over the
world for making this effort. And yet, why not live in our
landscape as it is?

'At present — and I can say this because I've spent
more time than most people out in the utter wilds,
looking for rare birds that have survived only in the bush
— it's a matter of preserving birds if we can. That's the
new movement of controlling rats and stoats in patches
of bush in places like Waitakere and Karori. If you do
enough of that you can have rare native birds, even
stitchbird and saddleback. But they won't survive unless
basic controls are carried out. On the whole, the birds
that are survivors are the ones that maybe matter ecologically.'

Turbott had been to so many offshore islands, and
now he was in a retirement village in Auckland with a
view of a phoenix palm. I asked about the birds around
him. He picked up his Pentax bins, looked out the
window, and said, 'There are thrush singing, fantail, grey

warbler in the garden next door. Just there, there's a blackbird in possession of that power box. He's whitewashed the top of it. About now they're beginning to stake out their territories, and getting quite aggressive for spring.

'About 30 or 40 mynahs roost in that palm. Better still, for two years I've watched kingfishers nesting just beneath them – they get in and make a small hole so the mynahs can't get at the chicks. Whatever helps native birds to get established is interesting.'

On my way out I lingered at the doorway. He suddenly thought of something, took off on those long, loping legs, came back and said, 'This was Bud's.' He held out a relic, a great big old torch that had belonged to Major Geoffrey Buddle, DSO, MC, Serbian Eagle. Would anyone mind too much if I said that he was carrying an eternal flame?

Nesting colony of
Caspian Terns on the
beach at Mangawai,
21.10.40

Dear Gwen

YOU CAN TELL a lot about a person by the way they receive someone else's good news. Not sure how to react, formal, mildly congratulatory — 'I'm so pleased.' Who knows what becomes of the half-hearted, but you don't really want to bother with people like that. When I told Gwenda Pulham the happiest news of my life, one evening when she picked me up to go to the monthly meeting of the Auckland OS, she fairly squawked with joy. I had a feeling she might. She doesn't do anything by halves, least of all from her heart.

I met Gwen on the first night I plucked up courage

to attend an OS meeting. It was held in a freezing cold lecture room on the Unitec campus. A two-dollar donation at the door, 21 people in attendance, tea-bag tea and malt biscuits upstairs in the kitchen. I wrapped myself up tight in an overcoat and listened to veteran ornithologist Dick Veitch give a talk about the crisis facing red knots in America's Delaware Bay. Yes, most interesting. Afterwards, notable bird sightings were shared. A white heron, the solitary kotuku, had been seen at the public toilets in Kaukapakapa on the Kaipara Harbour. Various other topics came up, and one voice interjected the most, opinionated and inquiring, always there with a question or a trenchant point of view. I thought: I must talk to her. This was Gwen, who became my closest birding friend.

After we had chatted that July night over the tea and the malt biscuits, she picked me up outside my flat three days later, and I spent an exhilarating afternoon with her among the wading birds on Omaha Spit. Her first words were: 'Aha. Got your bins. Good.' I learned quickly that birders were tremendously single-minded. They didn't waste time with talk of other things; life was some-thing that flitted in the background: they had eyes only for birds. Phil Hammond, one of New Zealand's few bona fide twitchers — birders actively and passionately engaged in sighting rare birds — told me once about tromping across Waikato farmland with two other twitchers in pursuit of the rare dunlin. One of the men had just had a successful triple bypass. 'Funny thing was,' Phil said, 'no one even mentioned it...'

Which is not to say that getting Gwen to talk about things other than birds was as hard as pulling teeth. Yes, yes, a deliberate metaphor: she works as a school dental technician. She had joined OS 30 years earlier, in 1976, wanting something to keep her mind and body fit. Other birders could certainly vouch for the latter: back then, as a younger woman with a most pleasing figure, she had caused something of a scandal when she showed up at beach expeditions wearing a bikini.

She made endemic birds her study, until, she said, something happened in the late 1980s: 'I saw the light!' Gwen became a 'wader', fascinated by and in thrall to New Zealand's migratory wading birds. Among our birders, waders are a kind of cult – possibly the most fervent of our modern ornithologists, followers of the true path. In part, it's an Auckland thing. The city has two harbours and is nearby to a third, the giant Kaipara, all of which attracts vast numbers of wading birds. Actually, the birds turn up all over the shop, at coasts and tidal estuaries in both the North and South Islands.

These migratory wading species have a special status. I deliberately left them out of the pecking order of New Zealand birds earlier, because they occupy such a distinct niche. New Zealand is a littoral nation – littoral, meaning shores. We are the land of the long white coast. Our shell banks, mud-flats, dunes, and above all our shuffling tides are ideal for a remarkable variety of wading birds. One of the great sights of bird-watching is huge flocks of wading birds mobbed together as they wait for the high tide to shuffle out.

Most wading birds are attractive, with their long legs and long bills. The pied stilt is probably the most graceful of all, the Kate Moss of birds, thin as pins and light as... well, feathers. But there is much more to wading birds than their looks. There is the fact of their migrations. Most birds are stuck here, day in, day out, but migrating waders have a romance about them, an emotional upheaval.

A few species migrate within New Zealand – such as wrybill, which take about six, seven hours to fly up from their Canterbury breeding spots to spend the summer in Auckland. Many other species are international, making epic journeys from the desolate Arctic tundras each season to winter in New Zealand. In her famous 1937 novel *The Godwits Fly*, Robin Hyde saw New Zealanders as godwits who 'must make the long migration, under a compulsion they hardly understand; or else be dissatisfied all their lives long'. Really? It's always absurd to talk of birds as humans, but the worst conceit of that observation is the 'compulsion they barely understand'. Godwits understand it quite well. It's a matter of life and death. Also, Hyde refers only to godwits leaving New Zealand. The fact is, godwits always return. They choose to come here.

On that cold day in July, Gwen led me across the dunes at Omaha. She stopped now and then to roll up a cigarette; no wonder we hung out together — she was the only birder I met who smoked. It began to rain, a stiff wind rose up, but Gwen was in bright spirits. It was the school holidays, and this was a precious chance for her to get out during the week. Soon, she had found what I wanted to see. That afternoon was the first time I ever laid eyes on a godwit.

Six of them, juveniles, content to stay in New Zealand over winter, long-legged, plump, and probing their long, sensitive bills into the tide line. Next autumn they might leave New Zealand on the mass, epic migration. They were a fabulous sight. It was, actually, a moving experience. I felt some kind of deep connection with the birding tribe now that I had seen a godwit. I thought of all the other eyes that had watched this bird, studied it, marvelled at it. As for the bird itself — a dull, scruffy thing, to be honest, but that wasn't any more the point than if it had been decked out in its vivid red breeding plumage. Again, even more deeply, I felt moved, and it was to lay eyes on a bird that lived half the year in just about the most remote part of the world, the Arctic, and the other half in the remoteness of these lazy sensual isles.

Also that day Gwen counted 61 New Zealand dotterels, already in their breeding stripes: 'If we're quiet,' whispered Gwen, 'we'll see copulation.' Among the flock at the tide was one wrybill, a fascinating little bird with its unique feature – it's the only bird in the world that has a bill that curves sideways, to the right. There are only an estimated 5000 wrybill in New Zealand, which is to say there are only an estimated 5000 wrybill in the world.

What a magnificent day that was. I felt like I had been introduced to another kind of New Zealand – a particular New Zealand geography, another kind of New Zealand history, a different New Zealand story. Godwit, dotterel, wrybill: now I had seen them, now I had looked at them long and swooningly through my bins and Gwen's scope, I felt changed, enriched.

For Gwen, it was just another opportunity to count. Keeping count is what birders do; numbers are their shared language. It's a vital exercise, because it keeps track of bird populations and movements. Her particular passion, though, was fairy terns. A rare and endangered species, there are less than 40 fairy terns remaining in New Zealand. (A chick on the Kaipara Harbour would later, in the summer of 2007, be successfully fledged and ready to fly, the first such event in five years.) Gwen's work to protect the fairy terns had won her the Queen's Service Medal. She told me something of her dramas. There was the day a fairy tern egg was about to be washed away by the tide, but she saved the unborn chick by placing the egg in a wide-necked soup flask. There was the day she staged a sit-in at the Department of Conservation offices.

And there was the fairy tern nest she found one day on the beach at Waipu. Like most shore birds, the fairy tern lays its eggs in a scrape in the sand. That night, there was a party on the beach, a bonfire, a game of cricket... She watched on helplessly, and got up at dawn to find a line in the sand – well bowled, sir – where the nest had been. 'I sunk to my knees and cried,' she told me. 'I thought, surely everyone has a right to raise a family.' Dear Gwen. Of course I knew she would be happy when I told her my news.

Caspian Tern chick,
four days old

Little wing

B Y NOW IT ought to be blaringly obvious – apologies for the coyness – what I have been getting at with so many hints, so much moist sentimental clucking, about something amazing that happened along the way during my year of birds. Emily phoned one morning while I was at my desk. I work from home. She had unexpected news. I said, 'Just come over!' I sat out on the back porch waiting for her. It was a warm, bright winter's day. I wept with happiness and smoked my head off. Emily arrived. She trembled with happiness. There was sunlight on her face. She said, 'Get that smoke away from me! I'm carrying our baby.'

Our baby. A new life, someone else, someone we hadn't planned, someone we wanted, and immediately, giddily, cherished. I thought: I love you, whoever you are. For the first time in my life I felt set free. I imagined our baby, and thought: you are my life. Please, take as much as you want.

Emily – suddenly, she was the mother of my child – went back to work. Dazed and amazed, suddenly fiercely protective, I wandered down to the bay. There were those other parents-in-waiting, the pair of white-faced herons – up to five pale blue-green eggs would hatch in the spring. On that winter's day, at high tide, they were in lazy flight, their long, supple necks tucked close to their chest. There were six pied shags and one little shag on the pier. It was true about the pied shags, that they dive underwater for 25 to 30 seconds, and rest for no longer than ten seconds before their next fishing trip.

Back home, sitting at my desk, I gazed at the silver-eyes scoffing every morsel of fruit on the guava tree outside my window. At head-height in the fork of a thin tree a few houses up the road, I found a thick nest, like a cup, very tightly made from twigs and dry grass – quite likely a goldfinch or chaffinch, which sometimes also raided the guavas.

Birds, everywhere, scattered all around, the air full of feathers and cries, a new kind of New Zealand emerging in front of my eyes as I wandered through the first tender and ecstatic days of Emily's news. I looked at the red, hard, almost reptilian feet of the red-billed gull; heard the blackbirds break their autumnal silence and begin to sing in late July; went to the zoo and was terribly pleased with myself for being able to identify non-captive yellowhammers eating the hayseeds thrown about by Fudge, the neutered hippo (and even more excited to notice that welcome swallows had moved in, and built a nest beneath a footbridge); and followed a flock of spur-winged plovers one afternoon across a damp field near the harbour bridge, in the hope of finding a nest. The *Field Guide* had said, 'Laying is from June till late November. Several clutches are laid each year. The preferred site is a flat, wet area with some surface irregularity and a wide outlook. The nest is a scrape in the ground. They lay 1 to 4 khaki eggs with brownish-black spots.'

There were more outings with Gwen, to that most alluring hotspot for a birder: a sewage pond. Lagoons and shell banks had been restored to the 500 hectares of dewatered sludge at the former oxidation ponds at Mangere, and were a haven for shore birds and waterfowl. We saw juvenile bar-tailed godwits, already showing a lovely red tint to their bodies in preparation for the breeding season. There were SIPOs and New Zealand dotterels.

'Look,' said Gwen, 'a scarf of wrybill.' She pointed out a flock of about 140 birds coming into land — wrybill really do fly in the shape of a scarf flung in the air. There were pied stilts. 'Look,' said Gwen, and among the flock of pied stilt at the water's edge, she picked out a solitary black stilt. The rare black stilt. There are only about 70 left in New Zealand, making it one of the most threatened shore birds in the world, according to British-based BirdLife International.

And there were what I had hoped to see at the ponds – royal spoonbill, one of the most striking birds in New Zealand, graceful with its long black legs, its snow-white, radiant plumage, and the way it flies with its neck stuck out, but made preposterous with that great big un-gainly spoon sticking out of its face. It's another modern self-introduced Australian bird, and began breeding here in 1947. There was a flock of 72 at Mangere. They waited for the tide to recede, until, one by one, they stalked into the water and spent a good 20 minutes bath-ing before feeding. It was moulting season; you could see a bloody red where the feathers were coming through. Most stood on the shell bank in classic wader pose, on one leg, but a few sat, folding their legs beneath them like a bundle of sticks.

Gwen and I sat watching the spoonbills nearby, nibbling at sandwiches and drinking thermos coffee provided by John Simmons, an OS member who had also come along for the day. John was 72 and another English birder; he had emigrated here with the wife and kids after giving up his job as a fireman with the Hertford-shire brigade. He said, 'They were mad down at the fire station. They said, "What are you going to do in New Zealand?" I said, "Milk at four cents a pint, I could live on rice puddings till I get myself sorted." But it turned out fine.'

After his wife passed away 12 years ago, he took up an interest in birds — in part, inspired by reading something in a book called *The Young Pathfinders Book of Birds*. When I phoned him later and asked him about the book, he said, 'I'm looking at it right now. Here we go: "Many birds eat particular foods, and go about their food-gathering in unusual ways. The chicken-sized kiwi of New Zealand delights in perhaps the strangest food of all. The kiwi loves to gobble a certain long phosphorescent worm. It doesn't seem to mind that the worm, 12 to 20 inches long, makes its whole bill glow like a light bulb. For a long while after the meal, until all the effects of the worm wear off, the kiwi's bill keeps glowing." The first time I read that I thought, that's going a bit far.'

John and Gwen shared the kind of dialogue only birders can speak. Example: 'Brian was asking me about the state of a spoonbill in my freezer.' They could perform endless varieties of these dead-bird sketches: John served as the Auckland OS beach patrol coordinator, in charge of volunteers who devoted one Saturday each month to combing 30-kilometre stretches of Muriwai Beach in search of storm-cast sea birds washed up on the shore. Six mottled petrels in March, 17 little blue penguins in August and another 15 the following May,

19 fairy prions in July. The death toll could sound enigmatic, like a line of verse separated from its poem:

10 sooty shearwaters in June.

Beach patrolling is crucial to OS work. Every year, thousands of dead sea birds fetch up on New Zealand beaches, providing the raw material, so to speak, for an understanding of migration. The beach patrols also allow particular study of population, age, anatomy, moult and feeding. It's a sub-genre of ornithology — how to watch a dead bird. Between 1943 and 1987, patrollers found 209,204 dead sea birds on the New Zealand coastline, as well as dead other things. John: 'Found a dead horse once. A month later, a dead deer. Three sheep's heads.'

Recent rare-bird finds included the brown-phased Oriental cuckoo from New Guinea, and the northern giant petrel, whose leg band traced it back to South Africa's Cape Town University, where the bird had been banded in 1984, making it at least 22 years old. John made sure every collected bird was properly, tightly Gladwrapped, then triple-bagged, and he took along two three-litre containers of hot water, plus detergent and hand towels. 'Some of the birds,' he said, 'are long past their use-by date.'

I can vouch that a dead sea bird stinks to a high, musky hell. One night, when Gwen drove me out to the South Auckland OS meeting at the croquet club-rooms, someone brought along a fairy prion. Its blue-black bill was at right angles, the top pointing left, the bottom pointing right, and a most interesting discussion ensued as to whether this was a freak mutation, or a car had run over it. Later, as a university research student gave a talk on the perplexing rate of breeding failure among the little blue penguin on Tiritiri Matangi Island, my mind kept wandering back to the fairy prion – partly because of its distinctive stink, but also because it was the closest I had ever been to a bird.

There are over a million pairs of fairy prions around New Zealand waters. They lay only one egg in season, in a burrow in the ground, where the eggs and chicks are hopelessly vulnerable to cats and rats – and also, on Stephens Island, to tuatara. All I really knew, though, was how tiny it was, this grey sea bird with a twisted bill and blue legs, all of it quite dead, inside a plastic shopping bag from Foodtown on a table in a croquet club-room in Papakura. It had felt hollowed out in my hand, almost weightless, as though it only contained sea salt and sea air.

I chatted to Ian Southey that night. A few days later he invited me out birding on the Kaipara Harbour; he picked me up one Sunday for a long and rewarding day on possibly the bleakest stretch of inland tide in the country. Fit and somewhere in his thirties, he advertised he meant business as soon as he parked the car, stripping down to a pair of shorts and bare feet, even though it was a cold winter's day, raked by a sea breeze.

Ian's list of species he had seen in his life was about 230; he didn't keep count, it wasn't his thing. He was a serious student of birds — that year he worked on the dunlin, and would later post an email on the popular BIRDING-NZ internet newsgroup, excitedly describing his Department of Conservation survey work on forest yellowheads in Otago's Dart River: 'You should be here!'

He brought along a spare scope to our day on the Kaipara, and we trudged for hours along a black damp tundra, stopping here and there to inspect and to count: 161 SIPOs, 125 bar-tailed godwits, 71 New Zealand dotterels, 61 banded dotterels, plus two species of Arctic breeders, probably juveniles, wintering in New Zealand — 25 orange-legged turnstones, and 541 knots.

The day included a rare find. Ian picked out the terek sandpiper, a voracious feeder with its delicately upturned bill. I smiled to see this scarce visitor to our shores, because I had just finished reading Mark Obascik's modern classic *The Big Year*, his captivating account of three US twitchers who fiercely competed to find the most species in North America in 1998. Towards the end of that year, the numbers were close. New Jersey industrial contractor Sandy Komino was on 703, retired chemical company executive Al Levantin had 663, and the dark horse, Greg Miller, a lonely, divorced, broke, overweight nuclear-power worker from Maryland, could count 658. Obascik: 'After a four-day, 6500-mile sweep of the Pacific Northwest, Komino returned home to a jarring phone call. Turn around right now and come back, the caller told him. There's a terek sandpiper working the surf in Anchorage.' Naturally, Komino did as he was told.

All that, just for one bird which fed its greedy face along the tideline on an unremarkable winter's day in the Kaipara Harbour, the distant tide holding its breath, the vast gloopy softness of mud-flats, at another end of the world.

A hen Bellbird,
Little Barrier,
25.2.48

Birdland

THE AIR WAS full of feathers and cries – all across the country. I began writing about birds in my weekly column in *Sunday*, and then asked readers what they had seen, and when, and where. They responded at length. The word count of emails added up to over 13,000, half the size of this book. A dozen or so readers also sent in those things written in pen and delivered in a stamped, if I have the word correctly, envelope. They came from south, north, east, west and Hamilton. They came from farmers, sailors, poets, politicians, pests, hippies, lawyers, scientists and exiled fans of Tottenham Hotspur. I was very grateful.

I read every word. They gave the pleasing illusion that 800 years after the first humans arrived, New Zealand was once again restored to its original state – birdland.

The findings? Birds mattered. Birds were important, vital, emblematic of an essential New Zealand happiness. Birds were right out in front, and the correspondents reported from a distance, in the background, fascinated and observant: the sorrows and joys of so many casual naturalists, compiling a record of bird life in New Zealand in 2006.

Some of it was useful. Glenda of Kawhia reported that in the past five years the population of royal spoonbills had increased from three to 25, and this year the harbour had also seen the first arrival of two white herons. Dianne of Whenuapai counted 27 sulphur-crested cockatoos (possibly the descendants of flocks reported in the late 1960s in Waingaro, or of a flock once smuggled into Port Levy and released from a ship) in a stand of trees in May, as well as two kookaburras – quite certainly the descendants of that strange nineteenth-century experiment when George Grey, New Zealand's two-time governor, transported wallabies and Australian birds to his home on Kawau Island.

Joan had sightings of Barbary doves on the lawn of the Philosophical Society in Orewa. Brian knew when 90 percent of the world's population of wrybills spend the high tide on the roof at Tranzrail's Otahuhu marshalling yards. Julia had a black fantail – the first she'd ever seen in many years of bush walking – flit from her shoulder to her head in a garden in Marlborough.

Corrine summoned the ghost of Major Geoffrey Buddle when she wrote of taking her elderly mother to the top of Sanatorium Hill in Cambridge every year from late August to late September, when tui (highest count, 19) come for the nectar of *Prunus campanulata*, or Taiwan cherry tree: the hill is named after the old TB sanatorium where Buddle made his recovery from gas poisoning in World War I. It was good to think of native birds gorging themselves on the spot where that old soldier came for his cure.

Robin, a commercial pilot from Christchurch, gave detailed sightings of 27 species, but was circumspect about the royal albatross: 'I have witness accounts of a colony, other than at Taiaroa Head, on the South Island mainland, which the farmer does not want DOC to know about for fear of having his land confiscated. I know the location of this site.'

There was a kind offer of expert help with this book from Amanda, a research assistant to an American Ph.D. student who had studied Pycroft's petrels on Lady Alice Island: 'Each evening we headed into the scrub carrying microphones to record the birds' vocalisations as they circled overhead, preparing to return to their burrows. We would hear little more than faint peeps in the dark … then an enormously unceremonious crashing as each one entered the foliage, hitting various layers on the way

down, and made our way to the source to find the bird
sitting silent and dazed enough to allow us within reaching distance. Eventually it would waddle in any number
of directions, at length finding its burrow, chasing the
tuataras out and slowly disappearing inside. Such a bird
could only have evolved with so little sense of its own
vulnerability in New Zealand.'

There was this strange anecdote from an enthusiastic
amateur, Melanie of Waiuku: 'Last summer, on the way
to visit my uncles in Nuhaka, we drove via the Waikare-
moana road. It was the most amazing scenery I'd seen.
We unfortunately came across a German lady who had
had an accident and her car was balanced on the side of a
300-foot drop, saved only by a small tree. My husband
and some other people tried to tow her out, and I walked
up the road to warn traffic as it was a blind corner. I stood
on this hill, and for as far as I could see was bush, and the
bird call was deafening – it was scenery you couldn't see
from the car. A large brown bird flew right in front of me
being chased by a bright green bird that was much smaller.
Only the day before, my husband had given me a book for
Christmas, *Birds of New Zealand: A Locality Guide* by
Stuart Chambers. I was able to confirm it was a long-tailed
cuckoo being chased by a yellow-crowned parakeet. I was
so excited...' This was literally a cliff-hanger: not a word
more on the fate of the unfortunate Frau.

Alan of Rodney rushed in with a wet blanket: 'Although a New Zealander, I spent more than 30 years

abroad, where I did most of my bird-watching. While NZ has many fascinating species, the harsh reality is that we live in an ornithological desert and I seldom go out walking with binoculars these days. I live on a 10-acre block where we have a good quality bush section with mature native trees. After two years here my bird list is a paltry 30 species, of which 16 are introduced – 10 natives and only four endemic species make up the list. I have seen nothing here that you would consider of interest for your book.' But then he cheered up – he was an OS beach patroller at Muriwai, which afforded rich pickings: 'It offers the chance of seeing (albeit dead) unusual birds that there is virtually no other way of seeing.' It moved him to poetry: 'Large birds, such as the albatrosses, are too heavy so we cut off the heads and only bring this back.'

There were missing birds. Mike Lee, chair of the Auckland Regional Council, sent in a copy of his doleful paper 'Failed attempts to reintroduce bellbirds to Waiheke Island', published in *Notornis* in 2005. The paper explained that 110 bellbirds were released on the island between 1988 and 1991. In late winter 1992, Lee skulked around the island with a playback tape of bellbirds singing. 'None were seen or heard.' A more intensive survey was carried out the following spring. 'None were seen or heard.' None were seen or heard by anyone on Waiheke by 1993. 'I note that most people don't write up their failures,' Lee remarked in his accompanying letter, 'which is a pity.'

There were dead birds. Jenny told of holding a song thrush that crashed into her window and died in her hand. Mites poured out of its feathers, then ran around her hand and up her arm: 'I dropped that thrush.' Penny told of the kereru that crashed into her windows with such force that 'they leave an imprint like a white angel. Must be the oil in their feathers.' In a sad sequel, she buried the dead birds in her citrus orchard, while a 'bereft' mate watched on from a rata tree. In a happy sequel, 'The resulting oranges are damn fine.'

Fortunately, there were live birds too. Joan of Tauranga: 'I knew that adult pukekos have the parrot method of pecking morsels from their foot while standing on one leg, but did you know that they often feed their young in the same manner, extending a foot clutching the food for the baby to help itself?' Denise of Hawera wrote about the 'uncountable number' of starlings roosting at the end of each summer in a belt of poplar trees running the length of her bull paddock: 'When they arrive in the early evening, they can cast shadows over the house ... The next morning at 7 a.m. – you could set your watch by this – they fly out in batches in a south-east direction.' She added a peculiarly New Zealand gothic touch: 'I have noticed that they won't fly over me when I am in the cowshed.'

More and more birds, live and dead, in more and more correspondence. My thanks to everyone who wrote in – the dozen or so birders, and the 200 or so raw, keen, unornithologised bird-watchers. A special gratitude to Rachel of Takaka, who emailed a short note about observing a flock of shags fly on to the beach from their nests on the Tata Islands. I wrote back with questions. She replied. I wrote back with more questions. She replied again. I found something especially appealing about the notion of those birds in that quiet corner of paradise.

She wrote, 'Tata is a small, sheltered beach that faces west across Golden Bay. There's no surf. The beach is on the west side of a slim peninsula, and on the other side there's a tidal lagoon. ... The shags assemble at dawn. When they get close to the beach, they fly down, put their feet out in front of them and ski in on the surface of the water. You can hear them land. Usually there are hundreds, and once we estimated there were several thousand packed close together. In small group after small group, they trundle back into the sea...

'Friends went round the islands at Tata in a canoe at Queen's Birthday weekend this year. One said that she'd been surprised to see the shags had chicks even in the middle of June, and that there were three hawks hovering over the nesting area.'

The soundless water, the leisurely canoe, the thousands of pied shags on a bird island — this was the acceptable version of New Zealand as birdland. Another, harsher version, marked by slaughter, tradition, work, money and an appalling tragedy, played out that year at the other end of the South Island.

Young Wandering
Albatross about
one year old

To kill a muttonbird

THE LAST BOAT BACK from the Muttonbird Islands harvest of 2006 was due to tie up at Bluff on a Wednesday afternoon in May. End of the season, the last muttonbird – the sooty shearwater – caught and killed, their salted bodies pickling in their own marinade of blood and oil, packed 20 at a time inside airtight plastic buckets.

What, said locals, you've never eaten a muttonbird? Oh, they said, you don't know what you're missing. The knowledge of it brought such pleasure. They beamed. They were thinking of more than just the meal of that boiled, reeking sea bird. It was the whole thing. The hunt, the work involved, the fun of it, the precious time with family on the islands – the tradition. The tradition which led to a tragedy at sea on 13 May, the deaths of six muttonbirders returning from Kaihuka Island, the boat so suddenly and so swiftly punched by freak waves and sunk. The tradition which led to a mass funeral, held on a warm blue day in Bluff, the shops closed 'due to a bereavement ... out of respect ... due to events'. The funeral began at 11 a.m. The streets were empty. The town was silent, motionless.

Five empty hearses drove along Gore Street at 10 a.m. towards the Topi house on Marine Parade to collect the bodies: Shain Topi-Tairi, nine; his cousin Sailor Trow-Topi, also nine; their grandfather, Peter Topi, 78; his daughter Tania Topi, 41. Family friend Clinton Woods, 34. The funeral of Ian Hayward, 52, had been held earlier in the week. The survivors – Paul Topi, 46, Dylan Topi, 16, and the *Kotuku*'s skipper, John Edminston, 56 – were joined by friends and family from across New Zealand, from around the world. They walked slowly, slowly, to and from the Topi house, cars lined up on both sides of the street, the sea at the doorstep of the Marine Parade house.

Actually, Bluff faces north, to Invercargill; homes up on the rise, beneath Bluff Hill, have clear views of the city lights at night. Like so many New Zealand harbour towns and cities, Bluff has its back to the sea. One of the best views of Foveaux Strait and Stewart Island is from the old cemetery on Lagan Street. It tells a brief history of Bluff: Bernard Lovett, drowned 1915; Arthur Light-foot, drowned 1913; James Waddel, drowned 1898; Andrew King, drowned 1894; Erasmus Duncan, drowned 1942. The cemetery also features a monument, a rock, dedicated to Bluff's founder, James Spencer. It reads, 'Died at sea. 1846.'

Any history of Bluff is a sea story. Its chapters record fishing tragedies. But what happened on 13 May 2006 was something archaic, singular, unto itself – a birding tragedy, a boat capsized in a notorious stretch of water, bringing death and grief to a corner of New Zealand that harvested sooty shearwaters.

How strange it was to hear people in Bluff refer to themselves as 'birders'. This wasn't the pleasant or obses-sive pastime of the white middle-class. This was the seasonal ritual of slaughtering birds. It wasn't bins and the *Field Guide* and pious talk of 'good conservation practices'; it was the fridge and the wringing of necks and pious talk of 'spiritual ancient practices'. You could say this was the real world, the seafood diet of see food and eat it. This was about birds as food, the moa disap-pearing into the 'Black Hole' theory of the human gob, the Maori harvests – banned in the twentieth century – of snaring tui, kaka and godwit for the pot. Quaintly, in August 2006, Dame Kiri Te Kanawa became patron of the Kereru Discovery Project, launched in an attempt to halt the population decline of the New Zealand pigeon;

politely, no one made any reference to the ongoing trapping of the pigeon for food, by Northland Maori in particular.

Europeans, too, ate their share and more, right from the start. When the *Endeavour* sailed into Mercury Bay in November 1769, the ship's naturalist, Joseph Banks, recorded: 'About 20 birds [pied shags] were soon killed, and soon broiled and eaten, everyone declaring that they were excellent food.' The introduction to the 1966 *Field Guide* comments on the colonial devastation of native species: 'Of course, uncontrolled shooting, based on the philosophy of the inexhaustible, contributed to the general decline. Wekas commonly went into the pot; kakas were esteemed a delicacy; and the *pièce de resistance* of a bushmen's feast might be a pig stuffed with native pigeons and tuis. The endemic ducks and plovers and native quail provided a tasty meal for hungry colonists ... In the Auckland Islands, shipwrecked mariners probably ate the merganser to the point of extinction.'

The weather was good that Saturday in May. Boats smaller than the *Kotuku* trawler were out fishing. The ferry service to Stewart Island carried on as usual. But in the afternoon an ebb tide was running, and when it goes against the wind, that can be bad, very bad – in a strong wind, waves in Foveaux Strait are almost vertical. The wind liable to cause the most damage is a north-wester.

It came around that afternoon, blowing maybe 25 or 30 knots, when the *Kotuku* picked up the Topi family from Kaihuka Island.

Peter Topi had gone out that morning by helicopter to help his daughter and grandkids off the island. The day before, he was up in Alexandra to attend the opening of a whare at the school. He was a hugely respected man, widely liked. He kept a good home on the island, and another one at Ruapuke Island, once the main Maori settlement in all of Southland, with its seven pas formed by the great chief Tuhawaiki, known as the King of the Bluff.

You could say that Ruapuke used to function as a centre of government; you could even say that now. Ruapuke Maori control all rights and access to the Muttonbird Islands. They were handed back by the Crown in 1997. Administrative committees were set up, by-laws drafted. This season was the first year that the islands operated under the new regime.

Morrie Trow, 73, sits on the committee. He wouldn't discuss the *Kotuku* tragedy — his brother had lost a grandchild, Sailor Trow-Topi. Neither would he discuss the tally of birds killed on the islands. That particular reticence was common in Bluff. Muttonbirding is a closed shop, not quite a secret society but a matter clearly of nobody else's business. 'To have the right to go to the Muttonbird Islands,' said Trow, 'you must be a descendant of the original owners of Ruapuke. That's where you get your rights from. You don't get your rights because you're a Maori. You might be a Maori and have lived in Bluff all your life. And your father, and your grandfather. But if your whakapapa doesn't go back to the original owner, you don't have the right to go. But I have. It's a blood thing. It's probably the last blood thing in this country.'

The tradition of muttonbirding is unique to Bluff. A unique source – the sooty shearwaters (estimated population, 20 million) make their annual migration from feeding sites in Japan, Alaska or California (at 40,000 miles, it's the longest migration ever recorded by electronic tracking) to breed only on the islands in the Foveaux. A unique set of customs – only the chicks are taken, either by reaching down into burrows and grabbing them out by hand or by hook, or getting them above ground, at night, when they come out and flap their wings about for the first time. The role of Maori, too, is unique, because the Ruapuke Maori include some of the whitest Maori you'll ever see.

'Oh yes,' said Trow, 'the Maoris down here have lighter skins than any other Maori in the country. They're no different to any other European in the country.' Trow looked rather like the actor Lloyd Bridges. His grandfather was a Shetland Islander. 'My grandmother was a half-caste Maori,' he said. 'We believe this is one of the first places in New Zealand that whalers and sealers really got into bed with the Maori. That's what happened

— they got friendly with the wahines, and then you had half-castes running around all over the place.' So, many Ruapuke Maori were Shetland Island Maori, Portuguese Maori, Norwegian Maori, Scottish Maori, Irish Maori. Their European descendants came to Bluff long before the Treaty of Waitangi — later signed on Ruapuke Island — and set up the town, naming its streets after rivers in Ireland. Trow could date his European ancestors in Bluff back to 1902.

As well as the tradition — Trow even claimed that muttonbirding was 'spiritual' — there is the money. Bluff muttonbirders freeze their catch and have enough to last until Christmas, or later. Many are given away as gifts, and to raffles. But you could ask around town and be told in whispers that most muttonbirds are sold in the North Island. About 250 muttonbirders are on the islands at any one time during the season, which officially opens on 1 May and lasts for less than a month, until the birds take off again on the long migration back to Antarctica.

It is possible for one person to bag a hundred, even two hundred or more, in a day. One bird fetches about $7. A bucket of 20 costs $170. Boats came back to Bluff with about 400 buckets from an island. As for the costs, there wouldn't be much change from $10,000 to charter boats and helicopters, and lay down supplies for the time spent on the island. But a good haul of birds might fetch as much as $60,000.

Private sales? You can get a beautiful feed of blue cod at the Bluff RSA for $14, but there wasn't a menu anywhere in town selling muttonbirds. You could ask, again in whispers, behind your hand. It might take only as long as the first person you approach. The kindness and generosity of Bluff people is legendary. One man said: I'll do you one. He said: Put your money away. He said: Happy to.

They said in Bluff: 'People are as welcome here as flowers in May.' Unless they came for the wrong reasons. The story of small New Zealand towns is told in pride; resentment comes when visitors are attracted by tragedy. It was one thing for the walls of the pubs to be covered in heroic photographs of boats riding enormous waves, and for murals to depict romantic shipwrecks of old (the *Scotia*, the *Okta*, the *Maid of Otago*). But the loss of six people, two of them children, was too recent, too private.

Too awful. There was a bit of a slop in the sea that afternoon. A swell. Everyone had seen worse. But a freak wave is exactly that: freak, no warning.

It would have been fast. The two waves that hit the *Kotuku* would have arrived right on top of each other. A minute? Probably 30 seconds. Not enough time to do anything, to grab life-jackets, to hit the radio. The first wave rocking the boat to the side, taking on God knows how much weight of water, the second wave finishing it off.

That was at about 2.30 p.m. No one knew anything had happened until crew on the regular 5 p.m. Stewart

Island ferry spotted buckets of muttonbirds floating in the water. The alarms sounded, search parties set out. It got dark. The big floodlights on the Stewart Island wharf were turned on. It didn't rain; it pissed down. It wasn't cold, it was freezing – for searchers out all night looking for bodies, it took them all the next day to thaw out.

Paul and Dylan Topi made the swim to Womens Island. A muttonbirder on that island had only just left for the season the day before; he could maybe have seen the *Kotuku* go down from his kitchen window. But there wasn't anyone around any more to help. Topi signalled an SOS on a torch. That was picked up, but he also wrapped rags around a branch, and lit it using kerosene he found in a hut. As well, he lit a fire on the ground.

Along with Edminston, the skipper, who had made it to the beach, they were picked up by helicopter and taken to hospital in Invercargill. It was too late for Woods. He had tried to find shelter; his body was found halfway up a cliff. Six dead. Three alive. Two funerals.

Maybe there's something in all that muttonbird oil, in its special pickle. At 73, Morrie Trow moved like a young buck, and his hair was full and thick; at 90, Harold Ashwell was as fit as any number of fiddles, his hearing unimpaired, everything in working order, and his stated aim was to go back out muttonbirding next season.

He talked about what you do once the bird is killed. 'First, you pluck them, and then heat-wax them to get rid of all the down. We used to boil them to do that, but waxing leaves a cleaner article. The head is offal. That's turfed. There was a time when the wings and hearts were kept, but not any more. Then you hang the bird, for at least 12 hours, and then slice it down the middle, and take its guts out, and dry-salt by hand − salting is an art in itself. You need only a fine coating of salt.

'Birding is like any sport − it gets in the blood, and you just can't stop. I love the islands. Everybody takes their families. We've taken our granddaughter when she was only ten days old. It's a good, healthy spot. No one ever catches the cold or anything like that. It's much warmer there than it is here. They tell us a warm current comes down from Australia and sweeps past the islands. I can believe it. At Christmas, you'd think it had snowed − all the trees flower, and there are so many white flowers that it's like a dusting on the island.'

He said his family had been birding since 1826: 'We're descendants of half-castes, really.' Originally, he said, muttonbirds were taken as food for winter for the family. And now? Oh, he didn't know what other people did with the birds.

Trow said, 'The demand far outstrips the supply.' This year wasn't a great season, he said. The birds were too skinny; when they eventually fattened up, the moon came out, and the birds stayed inside their burrows.

'Some seasons, the birds stay so skinny that when they leave, they're that sick and sorry, the first bit of bad weather they run into, they can't take it. You pick them up on the beach. This year you won't.

'This year, millions of healthy birds will have left the island. We already know we have sent away a beautiful bunch of birds. Next season,' he said, 'should be a great season for muttonbirding.'

Downy Bittern
chicks in the nest,
Papatoetoe, 18.12.38

Rare blue
chicken

TWITCHING IS THE new hunting. It's a genuine sport, with only a vague set of rules but a clear, ruthless purpose: to find as many rare or unusual bird species as possible. It's a genuine challenge – you have to act fast on information, and be prepared to travel a long way to an obscure patch of land. Time is limited, birds don't sit still. Numbers are everything. Scores are marked by lists – a year list, a life list, a world list, a national list, et cetera.

It's getting huge in Australia (a record 350 birders recently travelled vast distances to twitch a grey-headed lapwing that should have been in Thailand). It's already huge in Britain (one of the most famous twitches in UK birding history was in 1989, when 5000 twitchers descended on a supermarket car park in Kent to see the golden-winged warbler making its first appearance in Europe). And in America it's... very American, which is to say overblown, an epic enterprise, a whole continent to conquer, with events like the five-day Great Texas Birding Classic held in April, as well as the annual sea-to-shining-sea Big Year.

Overblown, maybe, but American twitching is high-end. A former record holder, Kenn Kaufman, described attending a speech by the great American birder Roger Tory Peterson thus: 'Listening, I realised he might have been any kind of artist. He might have been a composer, the great composer who began as a youth and learned to play all the instruments, who studies the intricacies of music theory, searching for musical perfection ... until he could sit down at the piano and improvise so brilliantly that every measure of music rolling forth from the keys would be an inspiration to the listener. So it was with Peterson, only it was birds, not music. Since his boyhood he had been watching birds, painting them, photographing them, writing about them, letting his quest for birds take him to all parts of the globe; now he could hold a room full of birders spellbound simply by reminiscing, by improvising. When it was over we would all be on our feet, rocking the room with applause – but while he spoke, no one made a sound.'

There are signs that twitching is the next big thing waiting to happen in New Zealand. Right now, it's the slowest next big thing. The record twitch so far attracted only about 20 birders – when an Australian reed warbler was at St Anne's Lagoon near Cheviot. I asked the man who is often described by birders as 'New Zealand's arch twitcher', Sav Saville of Feilding, how many serious twitchers there were here. 'I could count them on the fingers of one hand,' he said.

Four or five in the whole country! Twitching is a lonely business in New Zealand; the superbly named Robin Bush, who emigrated here from England (and whose bird photography is so good that OS members give him the ultimate accolade of saying he's 'another Geoff Moon'), talked to me about missing the camaraderie he was used to among twitchers back home.

Sav said, 'I can guarantee it will change. I just can't see it not happening.' This was partly said out of self-interest. Sav has a day job: it sounds like he's making it up, but he really is an air-force pilot. He has also created Wrybill Tours, which runs birding expeditions up and down the country. In fact, the first time I met Sav was last summer on the beach at Gisborne, when I was on my romantic East Coast trip with Emily, and saw a four-wheel drive marked WRYBILL TOURS. That car has done some considerable mileage in his quest for birds. Wrybill Tours operates pelagic tours – the Hauraki Gulf, the East Cape – in search of sea birds, as well as national tours of shore, forest and island, attracting international birders and hard-core twitchers on intense three-week trips.

As a destination, New Zealand is increasingly becoming a must-see birding hot spot, with British, European and United States birder companies raking in good money to bring twitchers our way. Sav: 'I looked at their itineraries and what they were achieving and realised we could do it much better from here. They just didn't know what they were talking about, really.' He set up Wrybill Tours with birding colleague Brent Stephenson in 2003, and figured it would take five years to generate any real business. 'But it took off like a mad thing. We made a small financial profit in the first year, and it's just gone completely weird. Turnover is approaching $100,000 this year.'

What's the appeal? Why come here to look at birds? You can see a greater, far more dazzling variety in other parts of the world. A fellow called Gunnar posted an email on Sav's newsgroup BIRDING-NZ, happily twittering on about seeing 500 species on a 12-day birding trip in Peru. It drew this very New Zealand response from a subscriber: 'Can someone please explain to me why anyone wants to see 500 bird species in 12 days? I have a big enough job finding, identifying, learning and remembering 150 Australian species in one holiday. I am totally exhausted by that number. Five hundred would be like ships passing in the night. At the end of it all would be only a dream, lost to the world of oblivion. I won't be going to Peru – that's for sure.'

Never mind the width, feel the quality. New Zealand has what Sav called 'high-quality birds'. He meant the species belonging to three bird families unique to New Zealand. First, and most obvious, the kiwis. Then the wattle birds – kokako, saddleback. And then the wrens – rifleman and rock wren. Nothing like them anywhere, and we also have birds only unto New Zealand (kea, kakapo, takahe, wrybill...).

How to watch a unique bird? The groundwork is in place. There are several other birding tour companies in New Zealand, including Manu, Driftwood, Kahurangi, and Kiwi Wildlife, plus localised tours to sanctuaries at Tiritiri Matangi Island, Kapiti Island, Mount Bruce, the white heron colony at Okarito, and albatrosses at Kaikoura and Taiaroa Head. As well, Greytown in the Wairarapa has a world-class birds store and gift shop, offering some magnificent antique prints – the US$350 print by nineteenth-century illustrator Frederick Nodder of the brown kiwi, gormless and impossibly upright, has to be seen to be disbelieved.

Now living in Tabor, Iowa, New Zealand birder Ross Silcock operates birding tours back home every two years – a 30-day blitz, including Stewart Island and Chatham Island, at US$7200 a head. He knows his stuff – the last trip, in 2005, clocked 162 bird species. By email, he wrote, 'My groups are a mixed bag. There is always a really gung-ho twitcher who wants to keep moving to the next spot, and gets upset if we miss any of the endemic birds.'

That reminded me of a story I heard from John Gale, former president of the Miranda Naturalists Trust. He picked up a Texan twitcher at Auckland airport, and drove him to Miranda. The twitcher had a sole purpose: he wanted to add a wrybill to his world list. The bird duly appeared. 'Aha,' said the twitcher, put a tick on his list, got John to confirm the sighting, and then showed no further interest in the wrybill. Or in any other of the thousands of birds at the shore that day. He'd seen those species in other parts of the world. They weren't on his list. Really, they didn't exist.

This is what makes true twitchers such rogues within the birding community — they're a rebel sect, wanting only to add to their precious, obsessive count. Not for these fellows — they're almost always men — the careful ornithological study, the useful activity (banding, beach patrols), the conservation effort. Those activities are strictly for the birders. And yet most birders are also closet twitchers. That day I was at Tupora in the Kaipara Harbour with Ian Southey, unseen by either of us responsible birder Phil Hammond was there too, guiltily relying on a tape recording of a fernbird to attract that secretive wetland bird his way. It worked, and the next weekend he was on an island in the Far North, twitching the nankeen kestrel, an uncommon Australian vagrant.

Wrybill Tours are keeping a record of birders with highest life lists of New Zealand species. Sav has 232 species, his wrybill partner Brent Stephenson 237. High scores were also reached by twitchers from other lands — Britain, Australia, the United States, South Africa, Canada, Germany, Holland. In second place, on 261: Colin Miskelly of the Department of Conservation. Top of the table: former Wildlife Service ranger and veteran OS regional representative, Brian Bell, who has 263 species.

When I spoke to Sav in August, he was making confident noises about being the first birder to score 200 in his year list. In the end, he was beaten by Stephenson, who counted 206, the last being a kookaburra in the Leigh Marine Reserve car park.

Well, you know what they say about records: they're there to be broken, toppled, smashed. What rough beast, slouching towards the brolga (an extremely rare Australian crane), is due to launch a challenge? Will anyone rise above the 300 life list, or more than 250 in one calendar year? The sky, obviously, is the limit.

As well as the native population to count and conquer, twitchers need to keep on their toes for visiting, or vagrant, birds. Birds from Australia, or Arctic waders caught up in other flocks — the lost, the windswept, the confused, the simply curious, the passengers who have hitched a ride on container ships. (Sometimes as stowaways on aircraft: Graham Turbott and Brian Gill looked into two cases of mangled barn owls that arrived in Auckland on international flights, the first dropping from the wheels and found by schoolgirl Sharon Richardson at Flat Bush School in 1983, the second almost exactly one year later in the undercarriage of Continental Airlines Flight C01 arriving from Los Angeles via Honolulu.)

BIRDING-NZ keeps subscribers informed of rare sightings. In 2006, messages included sightings of a single white heron at the Te Marua reservoir in Upper Hutt and another at the Waiatarua Reserve in Auckland ('Truly amazing... why aren't people talking about this?'), an unidentified Australian crane (either sarus or brolga) circling Moetapu Bay in Marlborough Sounds, a Japanese snipe at Forest Lake in Hamilton, a black kite near Renwick in Blenheim, eight cattle egrets on a dairy farm in Foxton, a long-wintering Hudsonian godwit at Miranda, and a glossy ibis wandering from Blenheim south to Christchurch.

There was also a white ibis, that extraordinary black-headed, white-plumed bird so common as a scavenger in the city parks of Sydney, sighted at Haast. This led to a raging debate about the Department of Conservation. DOC staff, who were first to spot the rare bird, were accused, then defended, of 'failing to disclose' the sighting to New Zealand's birders and twitchers. Comment from the anti-DOC side: 'Didn't you know that DOC has always had exclusive and confidential rights to New

Zealand's biota, and to most of its land too? It's only when they're short of cash ... that they break out with generosity.'

And so the ibis had unwittingly provoked a question – whose bird is it anyway? – which is bound to play itself out more and more in New Zealand's nascent twitching scene. The Department of Conservation is often viewed as the great killjoy of modern New Zealand life. The point of twitching is to go wherever there's a chance to sight a rare bird. It's false to say that armed combat awaits. But it's true to say that the pro- and anti-DOC factions settled on an uneasy truce on BIRDING-NZ.

Mostly, though, twitching here is marked by typical New Zealand amiability. There's an annual Twitchathon – teams have 24 hours, any day of the year, to rack up the highest count. The record is held by Ken Bond and Ted Wnorowski, who in 2006 sighted 100 New Zealand bird species in one day. Impressive. They covered a lot of ground. And it helped that they stayed overnight at the bird sanctuary on Tiritiri Matangi Island. This is what is known as twitching sitting ducks.

But almost every twitcher goes to Tiri. It's a fabulous place, beautifully restored, a masterpiece of conservation and preservation, and the star attraction is that near-mythical New Zealand bird brought back from beyond the grave – the takahe. I went to Tiri on a lovely day in August, walked along tracks through spectacular native bush, and happily saw saddlebacks, stitchbirds, tui, bellbirds, fantails, kokako, North Island robins, white-heads, red-crowned parakeets, and a pair of rare endemic brown teal, which slept in the sunshine by a pond, exactly like sitting ducks. Personal highlight? Takahe. Every New Zealander ought to see this bird. It's our superstar, our greatest survivor. It should be as celebrated as the kiwi.

The takahe came back from the grave not once, but twice. It was a food source for Maori at the same time as the moa, but the first that Europeans even knew it existed was when moa bones were discovered. When Richard Owen at the British Museum identified the moa in 1839, it caused a sensation. New Zealand collector Walter Mantell duly sent over crates of more bones, which included a shipment of a skull, bill and other parts of a skeleton of a different and unknown bird. Owen went to work, and was able to announce he had found another new species – the takahe.

It was assumed the bird had gone the way of the moa, and was extinct. But two years later, in 1849, Mantell bought a fresh takahe skin from sealers. They had followed the trail of a large bird in the snow in Dusky Bay: 'It ran with great speed, and upon being captured uttered loud screams, and fought and struggled violently; it was kept alive three or four days onboard the schooner and then killed, and the body roasted and ate by the crew, each partaking of the delicacy, which was declared to be delicious.'

Three more birds were caught and killed in the next few years. One ended up on Walter Buller's desk. Graham Turbott excised the following passage, which had appeared in the original 1883 volume of *Buller's Birds*, from his 1967 edition: 'On being introduced to this rara avis I experienced once again the old calm that always came over me when gazing upon the two examples in the British Museum – the lingering representative of a race coexistent in this land with the colossal moa! Then, retiring to the library, I shut myself in with the Notornis [Southern Bird], and handled my specimen with the loving tenderness of the naturalist.'

Quite. But the supply of takahe dried up, and the bird was once again written off, left for dead – until its dramatic rediscovery in 1948 by Invercargill ear specialist, Dr Geoffrey Orbell. As a child, Orbell had seen a photograph of a stuffed takahe. His mother told him it was extinct. Perhaps it isn't, he figured... When he tracked a takahe colony in Fiordland on 20 November 1948, Orbell – and the bird – became international celebrities, *Time* magazine describing the find as 'a state of ornithological ecstasy'. The bird was here to stay. Although easy meat for predators, superb conservation and recovery work has since brought the known population to about 250.

And so there it was, in front of my eyes on a winter's day on an island in the Hauraki Gulf, a bird whose rumoured death was twice greatly exaggerated, a bird whose existence shone with ancient history and modern miracle, now a tame kind of pet, not at all shy, an irascible picnic thief, huge and glowing and prehistoric, in full view on a grassy lawn, stalking about on two legs because that's all it could do, with a strong red bill, a fat blue head and a fat blue body. The most prized rediscovered bird in New Zealand looked for all the world like a rare blue chicken.

*A pair of White-
fronted Terns,
Tiri, 9.11.36*

The godwits fly

A PAIR OF SPOTTED doves roosted in a fig-tree in our back garden, and a neighbour's pet sulphur-crested cockatoo squawked out the words, 'Here, puss, puss, puss!' It was on a quiet street, the rent was good, and we held hands and spoke in whispers about the happiness that was waiting to enter the spare room. From the moment Emily and I moved in together, I thought: I never want to leave. We had arrived. Our baby was due in February. It was spring, and one of the first things I did was chop down a shoebox to the size of tray, nail it to a post, and fill it with wild bird seed for about 12 visiting chaffinches and the quiet pair of spotted doves.

Our arrival coincided with another, rather more outrageous spring migration — the arrival of the bar-tailed godwits and other Arctic wading birds back into New Zealand. An estimated 70,000 godwits were on their annual non-stop flight from their breeding grounds on the Siberian and Alaskan tundras, seven or eight days on the wing, until landing at shorelines in Spirits Bay, Miranda, Tauranga, Farewell Spit, Kawhia, Tasman Bay, Avon-Heathcote Estuary... All over, here for the summer, their fattened bodies turning red as bricks until they leave in March, although more than 10,000 juveniles stay behind. I went to Miranda in mid September. I wanted to see the new arrivals — I wanted a feeling of that incredible journey, surely the world's longest without resting on land or water.

Thomas Hardy, in *Tess of the d'Urbervilles*, had his own feeling about Arctic waders arriving in England: 'After this season of congealed dampness came a spell of dry frost, when strange birds from behind the North Pole began to arrive silently on the upland of Flintcombe-Ashe, gaunt spectral creatures with tragical eyes — eyes which had witnessed scenes of cataclysmal horror in inaccessible polar regions of a magnitude such as no human being had ever conceived, in curdling temperatures that no man could endure; which had beheld the crash of icebergs and the slide of snowhills by the shooting light of the Aurora; been half blinded by the whirl of colossal storms and terraqueous distortions; and retained the expression of feature that such scenes had engendered. These nameless birds came quite near Tess and Marian, but of all they had seen which humanity would never see, they brought no account.'

Terraqueous distortions! Genius. Poor show, though, that these 'nameless' birds had seen and done all that, and didn't have anything to say for themselves. Fortunately, Arctic waders have a voice in New Zealand, belonging to Adrian Riegen. When I was out on beaches and oxidation ponds with Gwen, she was always talking about Adrian this, Adrian that. Not entirely jokingly, she called him 'our guru' more than once. His continued work on wading birds is well-travelled — banding godwits in Alaska, and helping to set up a nature reserve at Yalu Jiang in China, where thousands of New Zealand godwits refuel on their northward migration — and wide-ranging, with special emphasis on the birds' migratory path.

Adrian is a classic New Zealand birder — from England, long and loping build, wears a beard. Very nice guy, with a sharp wit. He's also the practical sort; he works as a builder, and is adept at setting cannon-fired netting to catch wading birds on the beach. 'You get over a thousand birds, trapped and squashed, flapping away and people running in all directions ... It can look quite alarming.'

The closest I had been to a bird was the dead fairy prion one night at the Papakura croquet club. But I felt an almost physical sensation listening to Adrian describe his practised intimacy with birds – he has banded thousands of waders. 'Wrybills sit in your hand so easily. Oystercatchers are tough old birds, incredibly placid, but the only thing is that they crap all over you. With the godwits and knots, their bill may be long and pointed, but it's actually a very delicate bill, and they stress very easily.'

Adrian had the familiar bird-watchers' confession – 'I was a teenage twitcher' – but his interested widened, became seriously ornithological when he got hooked on waders in 1969. He said, 'It was seeing the buff-breasted sandpiper. These things should have been heading to the pampas in South America, and yet they were on these islands off the west coast of Cornwall. So I started read-ing more about waders and their fantastic migration. They're such a global species that wherever you go, you're going to find waders. And often they're the same species: you've got bar-tailed godwits and red knots here, but you also have them in Britain, America, South Africa, South America. The more you study these birds, you more you want to see where they go.

'With our bar-tailed godwits, we knew they bred in the Arctic, but how they got here, and how they got back, or which particular parts of the Arctic they used, we had no idea about really. The books said, "Oh, they go via Asia." Well, that's a fairly good guess. You didn't need to be too smart to figure that was probably the case. Once

we started banding the birds in the mid 80s, and getting
recoveries from Russia, and China, and so on, I started to
piece together the story.

'And you learn that the birds are under phenomenal
pressure in Asia when they stop there. People in New
Zealand just don't have any idea. You realise you could
easily lose things like the godwits and the knots if their
staging areas aren't protected.'

When I wrote my column in *Sunday* asking readers
to send their bird sightings or experiences, Christchurch
poet Jeffrey Paparoa Holman posted a letter enclosing an
article from the October 1961 issue of an inflight
magazine published by former New Zealand airline,
NAC. Amazingly, splendidly, the bar-tailed godwit was
the airline's symbol. The author of the magazine article?
'That old Huia swatter,' as Holman referred to him: Sir
Walter Buller. Lyrically, Buller described the godwits
departing from Spirits Bay in the Far North. He wrote,
'Just as the sun was dropping into the sea, an old male
uttered a strident call, and shot straight into the air,
followed by an incredible feathered multitude ... There
was something of the solemnity of a parting about it.'

Over a century later, Adrian was able to say Buller got
it right about the steep ascent, and the timing. 'It does
tend to be evening. Just literally on sunset. But they slip
away in littler groups, 20, 30, 40, maybe 50 birds, without
too much fanfare...'

Because I was off to Miranda in a few days time to

see the first godwits arrive for the summer, I asked about their landfall to New Zealand. He said, 'I was in Tauranga in October last year, and there were about 20, 30 godwits feeding at high tide, desperately looking for food everywhere, and dragging their wings along, which is a sign they had just arrived. They've had them held out for over a week, so when they land, of course, they can't fold them out, they're too stiff, and they wander around looking as though they've been shot. So we were looking at birds that morning which had arrived in the night after an 11,000-kilometre flight.

'And occasionally people have seen them land and not be able to stand up properly, almost like they're falling over. Generally, you don't see birds bird fall over, do you? But for the godwits, it's like getting their land legs back. They land, and their legs collapse under them. It's something you rarely see — you've got to be able to witness that initial landing, that very minute.'

I wasn't that lucky at Miranda. But it was a brilliant outing, led by Keith Woodley of the Miranda Shorebird Centre near Thames — how it grated on him that all the signs along that glimmering, white-shell shore stated 'SEABIRD COAST'. The point of Miranda and Thames was its shore birds, 43 species, with a summer population of about 200,000 waders. Keith was very nearly a classic New Zealand birder — long and loping build, wears a beard, but came from Invercargill. He's an accomplished artist. He lives in a house right next to the centre. It was a rather desolate spot, a sea breeze stirring the flax, and his only neighbours were birds; and yet, like me, he couldn't drive. He hosts 12,000 visitors a year. There is a lodge at the centre for overnight accommodation – the day I arrived, a merry group of Lionesses were drying dishes and making lewd jokes.

Keith walked me towards the shore. As a bonus, there was a single white heron, white and absolutely enormous, reaching to the sky on its slender black legs. I could add it to my year twitching list of the black stilt, the terek sandpiper, and a very weird sighting of an albino oystercatcher. Feeding on the tide were 300 wrybill, about 500 red knots, and 1500 to 1800 bar-tailed godwits.

The godwits were slim – they lose drastic amounts of body fat on the long voyage to New Zealand – and small, and slow, and dazed, and greedy. Their sensitive bills probed the sand for movement. They feed on crabs by shaking the legs off one by one, and then scoffing the body whole. For dessert, they eat the legs. They had come all this way – light, precious things that witnessed cataclysmal horror, curdling temperatures, terraqueous distortions, all the rest – and I stood and watched them on a white-shelled shore on a cold afternoon. It was Friday, 15 September.

I got home at about five that afternoon. 'I never want to leave,' I had thought, but that night I packed my bags, and left the next day to live in another country.

Immature
Blue Crane,
Goat Island,
Kawau, 9.12.36

In English

PINK-FOOTED GOOSE. Red-throated diver. Herring gull. Meadow pipit. 'Jay!' gasped Bill. A moment later: 'Oh. It's gone.' We were standing in a lovely copse at the Holkham country estate owned by the Earls of Leicester since 1534. It was so quiet. Soft autumn light fell on the stands of cedars and sweet chestnut trees. We passed by deer. There was a lake. And a sensational monument to Thomas William Coke (1754–1852), its base crowded with sculptures of bulls, sheep and a plough. The inscription declared: 'It imports posterity to know that he pre-eminently combined public services with private worth ... Love, honour and regret attend the father, friend and landlord.'

Egyptian goose, grey heron, great crested grebe. Bill had prepared a species checklist for the two days he acted as my bird guide in East Anglia and Norfolk. It contained 253 birds; he hoped we might find about 100, and we got near that figure on our merry field trip. Red-legged partridge, moorhen, ringed plover. I diligently ticked them off one by one, each time consulting my copy of *Birds of Britain and Europe*, published by the Royal Society for the Protection of Birds. Knot. Sanderling. Little stint.

Birds, everywhere, in an English sky – it was a dreamy couple of days, driving through that green and pleasant land, along narrow lanes and past flat fields, towards forests, woods, copses, marshes and the Norfolk coast. Kestrel, collared dove, goldcrest. We travelled from dawn to brittle dusk, the light falling at seven in the evening, every minute revealing England and England's birds.

But I was already dreamy. 'You all right?' Bill kept asking. I must have kept going quiet. My mind was so often faraway, on the other side of the world, on the other side of life. I hired Bill's professional services a few weeks after arriving to take up a journalism fellowship at Wolfson College in Cambridge University. I had won the fellowship as a prize. It was too good to turn down – a term in Cambridge, fed and watered and housed. But I longed to be home, longed to be by Emily's side. The day before I met Bill, she had sent an email showing the first scan of her baby. Our baby, with a face and arms; our baby, a girl, whom we called Minka.

'You all right?' asked Bill. I was more than all right. A girl – there were her arms, her legs; there was her face, and her lips and her eyes. Sandwich tern, greenshank, dunlin. There were a lot of beautiful and fascinating birds; I adored seeing the green woodpecker, and greater spotted woodpecker, sharp and vivid, battering at wood in the tops of branches. Beside a grain store at the side of the road, there was the frankly hilarious lapwing, with its long crest shooting out the back of its head. On a beach facing the bleak Atlantic, there was one dark, tough Arctic skua, which then turned and flew over the flat sea, its flight surprisingly long-winged and elegant.

My eyes were on the birds, the sea, and fields. My heart was on Minka. I wanted her to come here, to see everything I saw. She was on the other side of life – unborn, something taking shape. But already I was imagining her as a little girl, climbing on to the horns of the bulls of Thomas William Coke's preposterous monument, staring at the warm, dead body of a wood pigeon that I found on Sculthorpe Moor. And then as a young woman, her aged and boring papa escorting her around the fens and colleges of Cambridge. 'This is where I came for ten weeks while you were still in your mummy's tummy.' 'Yes. You told me,' she'd say, and exchange a look with her mother.

I kept saying her name: Minka. I wanted to talk to her, I wanted her with me. But I was with Bill. He was a nice man. He lived in London. He was married; his wife had two children to her first husband. The school they went to, he said, was rotten, typical of what had happened to England. I didn't know what he meant by that. I had no idea what had happened to England. I was just passing through, living in a house in a cul-de-sac called Barton Close with academics from around the world. I decorated the walls with wall posters of birds that came free in *The Guardian* and *The Daily Mail*. 'Birds,' said the vast Nigerian literary scholar who cooked odious pots of catfish each morning. 'Birds,' said the slender Italian political scientist who regularly phoned his mama at her home on Sardinia. 'Birds,' said the young Ghanaian historian who dreamed of drinking bottles of Star beer on the beach in Accra. We were all foreigners.

England was another country. Bill drove on through pretty East Anglia, each place-name like a grim comedy – Chalkpit Lane, Gong Lane, Grout Lane; Creake, Muckleton, Little Snoring, Wells-next-the-Sea, Sculthorpe Moor, Ickburgh, Gayton, Graunston. For the tourist, every day in England is a history lesson. You wonder about the centuries of peasants and kings, plough and smokestack. Birds, too, form the story of that island nation. There were the early myths, such as the 'robin miracle' of 530 AD, when Saint Kentigern performed the miracle of bringing back a dead robin to life; there was Shakespeare as the Swan of Avon, and Keats who wrote 'Ode to a Nightingale' after listening to that songbird under a plum tree in the spring of 1819.

The greatest names in early bird-watching are English. Even the great American bird illustrator, John James Audubon, needed to sail to England (via New Orleans, where he bought an alligator as a travelling companion, though it swelled to twice its size, 'breathed hard and died' after only nine days into the voyage) to publish his masterpiece, *The Birds of America*. By then, the lyrical prose of Gilbert White's *The Natural History of Selborne* in 1788, and the woodcuts of Thomas Bewick's 1797 *A History of British Birds*, had both brought about a revolution in thought, inspiring the first true wave of pursuing birds for pleasure.

Birds as sport and food had always been a favourite English pastime, and shooting birds to collect them as specimens was so popular that it had its own motto: 'What's shot's history; what's missed's mystery.' But the English have pioneered bird conservation. And the public have taken to birds in absurd numbers. A figure in *The Independent* claimed that bird-watching in England was a £250 million-a-year industry, bought into by an estimated 3.6 million bird lovers.

Approximately 3.5 million of them seemed to be at the bird reserves Titchwell and Cley during my visit with Bill. It was incredible. The car parks were full, and so were the paths towards the shoreline — you had to squeeze past lines and lines of people coming the other way with their bins and their scopes and their wind-cheaters and their walking boots and their thermoses and their packed lunches. It was like being on the London Underground. I was dying to be in the country, to escape to fresh air, but I was already there.

Little egret, dark-bellied goose, velvet scoter. Bill was racking up our bird count, and remained alert to any news of rare sightings: his beeper beeped all day long, courtesy of a 24/7 service that updated twitchers about movements and whereabouts. On our second afternoon, we parked near a thatched house flying a Jolly Roger flag in The Broads and joined a twitch of 12 birders to find a rare pallid harrier standing in a field. Old war stories were exchanged over the clicking of expensive cameras. 'I'm not fanatical,' a fat man was saying. 'I do it within reason. Although I was up in Scotland last Christmas. Ever so cold it was. I had three quilts on me and still couldn't sleep a wink. There were 400 people on that twitch. Ever such a crush, that was...'

The twitch for the pallid harrier was quiet and respectful. But I wondered whether any of the twitchers were among the guilty party who had been outed by the Royal Society for the Protection of Birds that same week. According to a story in *The Times*, a group of 30 twitchers had pursued a migrant rose-coloured starling to death in Norfolk. The bird had been blown off course in stormy weather to Great Yarmouth while migrating to India from Russia. 'They hounded him for two days solid,' said an RSPB member. 'I told them to leave him alone but they said "tough". It was tired and desperate to eat, but they wouldn't leave him alone. They weren't interested in its welfare. All they cared about was getting their picture.'

I got my 97 birds, ticked off on Bill's list, and returned with a bird feeder and a sack of nuts bought at the Cley reserve. Thanks to Bill, I was able to identify the birds that flocked around the feeder I stuck on the end of a metal pole outside my Barton Close house – blue tit, coal tit, great tit. It was good to observe them as the autumn days faded, and winter banged on England's door. Leaves fell from the trees, it got dark before four in the afternoon; I dozed in the warm, vast, silent university library while reading an original copy of Buller's book of New Zealand birds, dedicated to his sons Walter Leonard and Arthur Percival. Cambridge was such a loveliness, with its meadows and bicycles, its brilliant talk and its peculiar images, such as the topiary emperor penguin designed by Antarctic explorer Sir Vivian Fuchs in the grounds of Wolfson College.

Over breakfast, lunch and supper in the dining hall, I would try to keep up with the minds of fellow diners such as the Ibsen scholar from Norway, the giddy Swiss political scientist, and the Trinidadian engineer who claimed he was studying the vibrations made by musicians who played the steel drum. Much of the rest of the time, I plodded away writing a book, and tried to hide from the shame I felt after reading British ornithologist James Fisher's view on modern authors of bird books: 'Those who have tried it lately, under the misapprehension that nature writing still needs a Tone of Voice, or Slant of Pen, or (worst of all) a ponderous facetiousness, have not known what they were writing about, really.'

It was a strange three months. The food was good, the talk was amazing, the tits were pleasant on the eye. But I wanted to be home, where Emily slept while on the other, daylight side of the world I observed great tits, where the spare room waited for Minka. The closest I got to New Zealand was an afternoon in the basement of the Museum of Zoology, where I looked at Cambridge's collection of huia, stuffed and lying head to tail inside a sealed glass case. Just about the closest I got to England was the night in the Ffolkes Arms Hotel ('acquired by the Ffolkes family in 1678'), where I dined with Bill. The news in that day's paper was about Tony Blair finally declaring he would stand down as prime minister.

'Will you miss Blair?' I asked Bill. 'No,' he said. And then he talked about his own politics, about what had happened to England. He said he belonged to the British National Party. 'That's different from the National Front, obviously, I guess,' I said. 'Oh yes,' he said. 'They do their stuff in the streets. We keep it dignified.' He explained that its aim was to halt the wave of immigrants to England, which had lost its national identity, where hardly anyone at his kids' school spoke English, where hardly anyone observed or even knew of England's national day, St George's Day, where foreign cultures had become dominant, pervasive, out of control.

Ah, I thought. Here I am in the Ffolkes Arms Hotel in Norfolk with a xenophobic birder. What to make of him after he vented such a horrible little rage? He had looked so shifty when he gave that speech. But late the next day, on our way back to Cambridge, I put all my feelings of revulsion aside: he parked on a country lane, and said that perhaps, if we waited a few minutes, I might see something special. We hung around for about ten minutes. We trained our bins on the sky. And then, with a deep call to the east, something appeared – cranes. We saw these long, giant birds in flight, heads and legs outstretched, then land right in front of us, in a row, eleven of them, great big lanky birds, a thrilling arrival just before dusk, a few miles around the corner from a village that really was called Horsey. It was the closest I ever felt to England.

Red-billed Gulls,
Mokohinau

Summer

THE SUMMER OF 2007 – all that broad daylight making New Zealand once again the land of the long white page – was five royal spoonbills in Island Bay, a marsh sandpiper in Little Waihi, a wandering tatler among 35 turnstones near the seal colony in Kaikoura, a Baird's sandpiper at Lake Ellesmere, a Mongolian dotterel on Cow Island, a kookaburra on telegraph wires near Waiwera, a kaka mobbed by three tui in Albany, a sharp-tailed sandpiper on the Ashley river bed, a glossy ibis in Blenheim, a Hudsonian godwit at Port Waikato, and the channel-billed cuckoo was sighted on Motiti Island off

Mount Maunganui, then on telegraph wires near the roundabout at Bethlehem, and later feeding on a plum tree in Tauranga.

It was the season of the Australian vagrant flittering around on our shores. Birders and twitchers were out in force too, courtesy of Wrybill Tours, Driftwood Eco-Tours, Kiwi Wildlife Tours, Manu Tours and other guides, on board ocean pelagic tours, stalking the bush, inspecting wader counts, finding whatever they could find. Tourist numbers included nine Taiwanese birders, trooping along the hot January sands of Pakiri beach, weighed down with bins and scopes and cameras, and being led by a Kiwi Wildlife birding guide to a single pair of breeding fairy terns. A former English twitcher, now living in the Far North, notched his life list of New Zealand birds up to 187, and asked: 'Who keeps a world year list?' He had scored an amazing 920 birds in 2006.

Brent Stephenson of Wrybill Tours got his New Zealand record of 206 birds. It included positive ID of that bird given up for dead, the New Zealand storm petrel, in the Hauraki Gulf, a pectoral sandpiper at Miranda, a taiko in the Chatham Islands, a glossy ibis at Travis Wetland in Christchurch, a nankeen kestrel in the Far North, and bird number 193 was a rock wren in the snow – in December! – at the Homer Tunnel. It got him thinking about what would really be possible for a proper Big Year twitch in New Zealand, which is to say the remorseless pursuit of birds every day for 365 days, no expenses spared, throwing up in the sea one day and circling a sewage pond the next; he estimated a grand total of 255 birds.

For the less ambitious that summer, there were pleasures in locating a long-tailed cuckoo near Okere Falls, 2500 godwits at Karaka, and a weka swimming in Southland. There were special excitements. An Australian wood duck turned up at the Hokitika sewage ponds, although it eluded a party of nine British twitchers, and numerous attempts were made to confirm reports of a Japanese snipe at Whangamarino Wetland. Despite no accepted records of it appearing in New Zealand, there were rumours of a brown falcon chasing sparrows in the Far North; it was neither confirmed or denied that a stray leopard seal washed up in Fiordland, and scoffed five crested penguins; and there was some mystery about why SIPOs attacked over 100 fresh hay bales in a paddock in Southland. Other tales of common assault included pukekos killing two red-billed gull chicks at Sulphur Point in Rotorua; they were fed to juvenile pukekos, who ate the head and ignored the rest.

This was New Zealand measured by birds, the harvests of summer bringing birds to its shores and its forests, its river beds and its sewage ponds, its telegraph wires and its suburban backyards. Godwits had returned from Siberia to eat up large; wrybill moved up from the South Island to feed on Auckland harbours. When I returned from England, the thing that immediately struck me was New Zealand's lushness. It felt full to bursting. In my own backyard, song thrushes devoured a nashi pear tree in December and January, and silvereyes and spotted doves thrashed around in the fig-tree in February.

North of Auckland, at Ruakaka beach, a dune was roped off to protect a colony of New Zealand dotterels – their chicks had hatched, and scuttled across the sand like marbles. At other beaches and coves, SIPOs whizzed around my head whenever I unwittingly came too close to their young, and I watched a solitary godwit dunk its head under the tide to get at something with its long, sensitive bill.

Out at the Mangere oxidation ponds one day with Gwen, we saw approximately 1000 wrybill – a fifth of the world's entire population – plus 220 SIPOs, eleven little black shags, seven Caspian terns, and uncounted roosts of godwits. Two park rangers came by with good news. They had captured another two stoats, both females, their pained mouths opened to reveal the little sharp teeth that have annihilated New Zealand's bird populations for over a century. It was satisfying to look at the four deep grooves lodged in their back by the stoat trap, which is known as the George Foreman – when the trap comes down, it looks as though the stoats have been grilled.

Good. Birds, everywhere; that's what's wanted. It had been a year since the night of the black-backed gull flying past Emily's downtown balcony, a year since I first became aware of another kind of New Zealand — these bird islands, this birdland. It was full to bursting with a life I had never known about.

ACKNOWLEDGEMENTS

To Graham Turbott, Geoff Moon, Gwenda Pulham, Adrian Riegen, Brian Gill, Sav Saville, and John Simmons of the Ornithological Society of New Zealand (new members welcome) for their advice, patience and warmth. To the editor of *The Sunday Star-Times*, Cate Brett, for her indulgence, and to readers who responded to my bird columns in *Sunday* magazine. To John Naughton and Hilary Pennington at the Wolfson College Press Fellowship in Cambridge University for their support, and to Jaquelina Jimena, Massimo Ragnedda, Ital De-Valera Botchway, Sandrine Baume, Matt Edmonds, Luis Poulter, head porter David Luhrs and the kitchen staff at Wolfson College, where their friendship meant a lot during the writing of much of this book. To writers Neil Cross, Charlotte Grimshaw and Paula Morris for their literary encouragement. Above all, literally, to the swirling presence of birds, especially the white-faced heron.

BIBLIOGRAPHY

The 1826 Journal of John James Audobon: University of Oklahoma Press, 1967

99 New Zealand Birds, Don Hadden: Caxton Press, 1990

The Animals of New Zealand, Captain F.W. Hutton and James Drummond: Whitcombe and Tombs, 1923

The Big Year, Mark Obmascik: Doubleday, 2004

A Biology of Birds, Barrie Heather: Ornithological Society of New Zealand, 1966

Bird Islands of New Zealand, Robert Wilson: Whitcombe and Tombs, 1959

Bird Secrets, Major G.A. Buddle: Reed, 1951

Bird Watching and Bird Behaviour, Julian Huxley: Dobson, 1930

Birders: Tales of a Tribe, Mark Cocker: Viking, 2002

The Birds Around Us, R.H.D. Stidolph: Hedley's Bookshop Ltd, 1971

Birds in New Zealand, C.J.R. Robertson: Reed, 1974

Birds of New Zealand Locality Guide, Stuart Chambers: Arun Books, 2000

Birds of New Zealand, Alfred M. Bailey: Denver Museum of Natural History, 1955

Birds of the Water, Wood and Waste, Herbert Guthrie-Smith: Whitcombe and Tombs, 1927

A Book of Birds and Beasts, Dorothy Margaret Stuart: Methuen, 1957

Buller's Birds of New Zealand, ed. E.G. Turbott: Whitcombe and Tombs, 1967

Extinct Birds of New Zealand, Alan Tennyson and Paul Martinson: Te Papa Press, 2006

Field Guide to the Birds of New Zealand, Barrie Heather and Hugh Robertson: Oxford University Press, 1997; revised edition: Penguin, 2005

A Field Guide to the Birds of New Zealand, R.A. Falla, R.B. Sibson and E.G. Turbott: Collins, 1966

Focus on New Zealand Birds, Geoff Moon: Cameo Press, 1957

In Search of Birds in New Zealand, Ross McKenzie: Reed, 1972

A History of the Birds of New Zealand, Sir Walter Buller: Cambridge University library copy, 1888

The Life Histories of New Zealand Birds, Edgar Stead: Search Publishing, 1932

The Life of the Robin, David Lack: Pelican, 1953

More New Zealand Bird Portraits, M.F. Soper: Whitcombe and Tombs, 1965

Native Birds in New Zealand, Charles Masefield: Reed, 1948

New Zealand Bird Life, E.G. Turbott: Reed, 1947

New Zealand Birds and How to Identify Them, Pérrine Moncrieff: Whitcombe and Tombs, 1923

New Zealand Birds in Focus, Geoff Moon: Reed, 2005

New Zealand Birds, W.R.B. Oliver: Fine Arts, 1930

New Zealand Land of Birds, Geoff Moon: New Holland, 2001

Notornis, Volumes 1–52, 1940–2006

Paintings of the Birds of New Zealand, J.G. Keulemans: Random House, 2006

Pyramid Valley, Roger Duff: Pegasus Press, 1952

RSPB Birds of Britain and Europe, Rob Hume: Dorling Kindersley, 2002

The Shell Bird Book, James Fisher: Ebury Press, 1966

This Birding Life, Stephen Moss: Aurum Press, 2006

The Travelling Naturalist Around New Zealand, Brian Parkinson: Century Hutchinson, 1989